CHARLIE – AN UNWANTED CHILD?

IN SEARCH OF A THERAPIST

Series Editors: Michael Jacobs and Moira Walker

CHARLIE – AN UNWANTED CHILD?

Edited by Michael Jacobs

OPEN UNIVERSITY PRESS
Buckingham • *Philadelphia*

Open University Press
Celtic Court
22 Ballmoor
Buckingham
MK18 1XW

and

1900 Frost Road, Suite 101
Bristol, PA 19007, USA

First Published 1995

A catalogue record of this book is available from the British Library

ISBN 0335 19199 1 (pb)

Library of Congress Cataloging-in-Publication Data

Charlie – an unwanted child? / edited by Michael Jacobs.
     p.   cm. — (In search of a therapist)
     Includes bibliographical references and index.
     ISBN 0–335–19199–1
     1. Psychotherapy — Case studies.   I. Jacobs. Michael, 1941– .
II. Series.
     RC465.C433   1995
     616.89'14—dc20
                                  94–29010
                                    CIP

Typeset by Graphicraft Typesetters, Hong Kong
Printed in Great Britain by St Edmundsbury Press,
Bury St Edmunds, Suffolk

CONTENTS

THE EDITOR AND CONTRIBUTORS

Cassie Cooper took her first degree in sociology at Birmingham University. She moved to London as manager for the Soncino Press. Later she took a psychology degree at Birkbeck College, and had personal analysis and formal Kleinian analytic training at the Tavistock Institute. She works in student health at Harrow, is a director of counselling courses and supervises several outstanding counsellors and therapists. She is a registered psychotherapist with UKCP.

Phil Lapworth, registered integrative psychotherapist (UKCP), accredited counsellor (BAC), certified clinical transactional analyst (ITAA), is an individual and group psychotherapist and supervisor in private practice in Bath. He has written and co-authored several articles and chapters on various aspects of psychotherapy and co-authored books on transactional analysis and gestalt counselling.

Frank Margison is a consultant psychotherapist in Manchester. He trained in Manchester in psychodynamic psychotherapy, where he was also a psychiatry lecturer researching in psychotherapy and the mother–baby relationship. He coordinates the local advanced psychotherapy training, and is the Honorary Secretary of the Psychotherapy Section of the Royal College of Psychiatrists.

Alix Pirani MA (Cantab), MA (HumPsych) has been practising humanistic and transpersonal psychotherapy in London, Bath and Bristol since 1974, after 25 years in education. She is involved in training therapists, and conducts public workshops and seminars in the UK and abroad. Her published work includes theoretical and imaginative writing.

Anthony Ryle read medicine at Oxford, and was a member of the Caversham Centre Group Practice for twelve years before becoming the first Director of the University of Sussex Health Service in 1976. In 1982, he was appointed Consultant Psychotherapist at St Thomas's Hospital, London, where he worked full-time until his semi-retirement in 1992, developing cognitive analytic therapy. He remains a Senior Research Fellow at Guy's Hospital.

Claire Wintram has qualifications in modern languages, teaching and social work. She has completed courses in bereavement counselling, rape counselling and counselling of people wishing to trace birth parents. She has worked in statutory settings in education and social work for twenty years, always with some involvement with adult learning. Since 1979 she has been involved in working with women, and since 1991 she has been working as an independent trainer and group worker, concentrating on all aspects of women's lives.

Michael Jacobs is Director of the Psychotherapy and Counselling Certificate Programme at the University of Leicester, a psychotherapist registered with the UK Council for Psychotherapy and a member of the British Association of Counselling. Apart from his clinical practice, he also writes on counselling and psychotherapy, being especially known for *The Presenting Past* (Open University Press) and *Psychodynamic Counselling in Action* (Sage).

And Charlie, whose contribution forms the core of this book, has for obvious reasons to remain anonymous, although much of her life story is told in full in these pages.

MICHAEL JACOBS AND MOIRA WALKER

SERIES EDITORS' PREFACE

Take five clients, and for each client take six therapists. How will the therapists, or in one case the supervisors as well, understand and work with the following situations?

Charlie is a 40-year-old secretary to a Trades Union official, married with three children:

> I think of myself as someone who lacks self-confidence and feels she always has to apologize for herself, and I'm very insecure. The mildest row with my husband and I think he's going to leave me, and he finds that very irritating, I think. Understandably. I would. Having thought about it, I blame my mother for that. I use the word 'blame' quite consciously, because all the while I very much got the impression when I was young that she didn't love me and doesn't love me. I think of myself as unlovable.

Jitendra is a male Indian psychiatrist, separated from his Irish wife:

> One thing that . . . interests me and sometimes worries me is my early years, my childhood years. I have very few memories of anything before the age of six or five, but I am sure that they have left some legacy behind, a significant legacy, and sometimes I have deep feelings of sadness or complexity or ambivalence which are not immediately ascribable to events happening around me. And I wonder what these . . . what this augurs? I think a therapist might . . . help me in this area. The other area that I am wanting to understand is the dynamics of a large extended family . . . I would like to understand a little bit more about what affects a person's growing up in that context.

Morag is an accountant, the director of a catering business, a mother, stepmother and partner:

> I feel that James wants me to be in the house, to be there because his children are there, and the family's there. He's quite happy to go off and play rugby on Sunday but he likes me being there, being the mother-hen . . . I get quite cross, that he keeps trying to push me into the traditional role. I don't feel I've got on as far as I could have done had I been a man, because I had to work twice as hard as everybody else to get where I got, . . . I feel OK always wanting to do something, but it does seem to cause quite a lot of conflict in my life. I feel, 'Is it right that I should always be wanting something new to go at, some new challenge? Should I just be accepting the way I am?'

Peta is an unemployed art teacher living in London:

> I've got a problem with men. At least that's the way that I conceptualize it for the moment. I don't know whether it's a problem with other things as well, but over the last few weeks, particularly – which is a different thing from deep background, I suppose you'd say – some issues seem to have come into my mind that are to do with the fact that I am a woman and they men . . . It's rather difficult to know where to start, except that I feel very self-conscious and rather uncomfortable about the fact that I must also tell you that I'm a feminist. And also that my father was emotionally very distant.

Ruth was abused as a young girl. She wants to hold her male therapist. What can he say when she says to him:

> Your reaction was – or I perceived it as being – a stand-off, and be cold to it, and not let anything happen, which obviously I understand; but I think it just highlighted that my desire . . . is not going to be matched by anyone else's. How can I communicate where I'm at, and help somebody else to understand that, and not necessarily to capitulate to me but just to be understanding?

This unique series of books takes a client's story, his or her presenting difficulties, the current situation, and some of the history from an initial session, recorded verbatim and printed in full for the reader to use. The session has in each case been presented to six different therapists. They address their questions to the client, and explain in each book how they understand the client, how they

want to work with the client, what further information they requested, and in the light of what they know, how they forecast the
course of therapy. The reader is presented with six possible interpretations and working methods to compare and contrast, with a final
telling response from the client and the editor on each of the six
therapists.

This series takes a further step forward from the comparative approaches of Rogers and others on film, or the shorter case vignettes
in the *British Journal of Psychotherapy*, which have both been de-
servedly so popular with students and practitioners alike. All the
therapists start with precisely the same information, which comes
from a largely non-directed initial hour with four real clients. The
reader can see in detail how each therapist takes it from there. How
they share similar and contrasting insights and interpretations of
the same person proves a remarkable and fascinating study of how
different therapists work.

The final volume in the series goes a step further and submits one
session of the editor's work with a long-term client to six different
supervisors. How do they interpret the verbatim material? What
questions do they want to ask the therapist? How do they advise the
therapist to proceed? In this detailed insight into the work of a
therapist and supervisors from different orientations, the reader gets
an in-depth view of the value of supervision.

The five volumes in the series are entitled *Charlie – An Unwanted
Child?, Peta – A Feminist's Problem with Men, Morag – Myself or Mother-
hen?, Jitendra – Lost Connections* and, finally, *In Search of Supervision*.

THE EDITORS

IN SEARCH OF THE CLIENT

Just how different is the approach used by a therapist from one particular training society from that of a therapist from another orientation? In recent years, there has been much more interest in comparing approaches than in competing approaches. It is sometimes suggested that different methods may suit different clients, or even that therapists tend to select out the clients they can best work with.

There have been other attempts to demonstrate the way in which therapists from different schools might work with the same client. For many years, the two series of short films *Three Approaches to Psychotherapy*, the first made with Rogers, Perls and Ellis and the client 'Gloria', and the second with Rogers, Shostrom and Lazarus and the client 'Kathy', were well used in counselling training. Raymond Corsini tried a similar comparison in print, in the book *Five Therapists and a Client* (F.E. Peacock Publishing, Itasca, IL, 1991), although in our opinion his book is marred by several weaknesses. In the first place, the client is a fictional case, and the first session therefore written entirely from Corsini's imagination – drawing presumably on clients he has known. Second, there are inconsistencies even within the first session, making the case less plausible. Third, each of the responding therapists is asked to imagine how the therapy would go, similarly writing their own dialogue. This gives them *carte blanche* to develop the case along the lines they want their therapy to pursue, which demonstrates the validity of their approach, and in each case ends up with success for their method with the client.

We wanted to approach the question of how different therapists might work with the same client from yet another angle. We wanted a real client, not a fictional situation as in Corsini's work, but more perhaps as Gloria and Kathy were in the sessions recorded with

Rogers and other therapists. In this series, we wanted to preserve the anonymity of the client, which a video or film cannot do. We also wanted to avoid what we believe inevitably happened in *Three Approaches to Psychotherapy*. The client is seen by three therapists in turn, but may be influenced in her responses to the second and third by what has happened in previous interview(s). We wanted all the therapists to start with precisely the same information, and to see how they might take it from there. In this introduction, we explain how we went about that and subsequent parts of the task.

Finding the clients

We used various contacts throughout the country to identify potential participants in the project, providing an outline of the method to be used. We invited applications from people who had never been in therapy before, since we wanted to avoid the contamination of their material by what might otherwise have been influenced from a previous therapist's interpretations. As it turned out, we learned rather late in the day that one of the clients had had a very short period of counselling with a person-centred counsellor, but over a rather different presenting issue to the one she brought to her first session with us.

After meeting those who were interested, and explaining to them the method and the safety features which we describe in more detail below, we invited them to return a consent form if they wished to continue. Their consent did not bind them to take part, until the point at which they finally agreed to release the material that had been taped in the first session. They could withdraw at any moment up to that point at which the therapists would receive their material, and were therefore committed to work on it. We, for our part, promised absolute confidentiality and anonymity (not even the publishers would know their names and addresses), and control by the clients over any material which could lead to identification. We also asked the clients to accept that we could not take them on for therapy, and that we could not be held responsible for their therapy, although we would endeavour to find them the most appropriate therapy if, during the course of our contact with them throughout the project, they so desired it. We also made it clear that we might not use their material, since we would be seeing more people than the series could use.

Several potential candidates dropped out at this stage. Seven people responded that they wished to participate, and between us we arranged to meet those who agreed to take part for an initial interview.

We arranged to meet for up to an hour, recording the interviews. We told them as we started that we would say very little, except to prompt them to say a little more where we felt they might value such a response. Some were more fluent than others, but we hope that we did not over-influence the course of the interviews. It was to be the client's agenda which each presented to us, and through us, to their six therapists. Our own interventions are recorded word for word in the record of the first session.

Of the seven interviews, three proved unsuitable for use in the project. All three were as interesting as those we finally chose, but two of them proved too similar as presenting issues to another which we already hoped to use. The third interview concerned us both because of the age of the client, and also because our understanding of the material concerned us. We felt it wiser to leave the client with natural defences. We had to be as sure as we could be from one non-directed interview that our client would survive any of the stresses that might arise in the course of such a project.

We ended up with four tapes from which to work, and we checked with the four clients that they still wanted to proceed before we transcribed the tapes. The second chapter of each volume in the series is a word-for-word transcript of the first interview. The only changes that have been made are to certain possible identifying features. These have been altered with the agreement and with the assistance of the client. The alterations made were internally consistent with the client's presenting story.

Once the transcript was prepared, it was sent to the client to be checked, particularly with regard to any further alterations necessary to disguise actual identity. We did not allow the client to change his or her mind about what had been said, unless to facilitate a disguise of identity, or where there was a clear typing error. Once more we made it clear that the client could withdraw from the project if he or she wished to. Only if the client was completely satisfied with the account to be sent to the therapists, and which would form the key chapter of the book, was the client then asked to assign the copyright of the material to the editors.

Finding therapists

Simultaneously, we started to look for therapists who could represent, at least in their theoretical position, the different approaches we wished to include in each volume. We wanted to find distinct methods or schools for each client, and where possible to have three male and three female therapists. Taking the first four books in the series together, we hoped to represent every major school of therapy. Suggestions were gathered from our own contacts, and therapists who were unable to accept an invitation were asked to suggest a colleague who might. In some cases we asked a professional society to nominate one of its members.

For the most part our task went smoothly enough, and the response we had was encouraging. Many of those who accepted our invitation quite rightly had one major reservation, that their work with clients depended partly (or in some cases largely) upon the face-to-face relationship, and working with its nuances. They accepted that in this case it was impossible to have that particularly subjective experience informing their work, although some more directly than others asked for our own observations, feelings and intuition in some of the questions they asked of us. This concern – a lack of direct contact with the client – was also given as the reason why some of those we approached to represent psychoanalytic psychotherapy turned down our invitation. This was the most difficult space to fill, although other reasons were also given, each one genuine in its own way. We began to wonder whether there was some resistance from therapists in this orientation to 'going public'. But perhaps it was pure coincidence that we had no such problems with any of the other therapies, including other psychodynamic approaches. We occasionally had a refusal, but nearly always with the suggestion of someone else we might ask, who then accepted.

Responding to the client

Our therapists were told, in the original invitation, that having read the material they would have the opportunity to ask further questions of the client, through us the editors. We felt that it would be disruptive for the client to meet each of the six therapists in turn, and that it would make the chances of identification rather greater, since it has remained the case that only the editors know who the clients really are. We were also concerned that we should continue to monitor what was happening for the client in the whole process. This is a person's life and story that we all have responsibility for, and while we wished the therapists to be totally honest, we also wished to ensure the clients survived, without unnecessary damage to them.

The therapists were therefore invited to ask for further information in order to address the headings we had suggested to them for their chapters to be consistent with one another. We all recognized, on both sides, that therapists would not bluntly ask questions of a client, but that some would take a life history early on, while others would expect such information to emerge during the course of therapy. We had to assume that there was certain information each therapist would hope to receive before the end of therapy. We were unprepared for just how much the therapists wanted to ask, and what we had thought would be a simple second interview proved to be more arduous and searching than either we or the clients could have imagined.

Most of the therapists sent long lists of areas they wished to explore further. Some sent questionnaires or psychometric tests. They asked in some cases for drawings, or for our own personal responses to the client. We were both involved in the Social Atom Exercise in Morag's case, one as director, the other as recorder. We collated the sets of questions so that they could be asked in a more or less natural sequence, putting questions from different therapists about particular aspects of the client's life or history in the same section of the interview, or where they were nearly identical asking them together. Although the therapists only received back the information for which they had clearly asked, where questions were almost the same, they received the same material and a reprint of the other therapist's question. Similar areas were addressed, but very few questions were actually close enough to be asked together. In a few instances, where the client referred back to an answer already given to one therapist, we supplied that information as necessary to a second therapist whose question had evoked this reference.

The interviews with our clients at this stage took several hours – we met at least twice, and in two cases three times. We carefully monitored how much each client could take, and asked periodically how much more he or she wanted to answer in that session. The questions were often searching and they sometimes gave rise to painful feelings and uncomfortable memories, although our experience was that none of the clients found this anti-therapeutic. They and we were stretched more than we might have anticipated, and we valued the immense thoughtfulness which the therapists had put into their questions, and the clients put into their answers.

Inevitably, there was a long gap between the first interview and this subsequent series of separate interviews, which took place much closer together. The original problems may have shifted a little, sometimes being slightly less troubling, sometimes slightly more so. The time lapse did not otherwise have much significance, except in the thought which each client had given to his or her own original material in the intervening period. Their own silent working on this material probably made their responses to the questions rather more full. Certainly many thousands of words were transcribed in each case, once again for the agreement of the client, before being sent off to the individual therapists. In all but one instance, the client was seen by the same person throughout. In Morag's case, her original interview was with Michael. To share the task of editing the four client volumes, it was necessary for her to be allocated to Moira for the second and subsequent interviews and collation of material, although, as already indicated, it rounded the second set of interviews off well for both to be involved in her Social Atom Exercise.

The therapists' task

The therapists' brief was to use the original material and supplementary information which they received from their questions and other 'tests' or questionnaires, to write an assessment of the client along the following lines, which form the main headings of each chapter.

1 A brief description of their own training background, and their therapeutic approach. Even though they are known to represent particular orientations (e.g. person-centred), we recognize that each therapist has particular ways of working, which might draw upon aspects of other approaches. What is important is to see how an actual therapist rather than a theoretical therapy works in practice.

2 The second section consists of the further questions which the therapist asked of the client through the editor therapist, and the responses they feel are relevant to their understanding of the client. Phrases such as 'When I met the client' refer to meeting the client via the editor. For reasons that have been explained already, none of the therapists made contact with or spoke directly to the clients.

3 The therapist's assessment of and reaction to the client – how he or she understands the client and the material the client has presented. This takes different forms, in line with the particular therapeutic approach, empathic identification with the client, counter-transference towards the client, etc. The therapists have been asked to provide indications or evidence of how they arrived at any formulation they might make, even if it is inevitably somewhat speculative.

4 The next section outlines therapeutic possibilities – indications and contra-indications in the client and in the therapist/therapy, in that it may or may not be helpful for that particular client.

5 The fifth section hypothesizes the course of therapy – what form it might take, the methods, the contract, the theoretical approach

in practice, and any shifts in approach that might be necessary to accommodate the particular client.

6 Next the therapist suggests possible problem areas and how they might be resolved. We have asked that potential difficulties are faced and not given a favourable gloss if it seems the client might not prove amenable to some aspects of a particular approach.

7 The therapist was asked to explain his or her criteria for success in this case and to try to predict how far these may be met. Aware of the positive outcome in all Corsini's therapists' accounts, we asked the therapists not to predict a totally positive outcome if they had any doubts about it.

8 Each therapist concludes with a short summary and a short reading list for those interested in pursuing his or her approach.

The final stage

As the therapists returned their assessments of the client, and their accounts of how they would work with him or her, these were passed over to the client to read. When all six assessments and accounts had been received, we met with the client for a penultimate session, to discuss the content of the final chapter together, before the editor wrote it. While it had been generally obvious throughout just how much the clients had gained from the process, their own final assessment both of the therapists and of the process is therefore available at the end of each book. We intend to meet with them one more time, when the book is published, to complete our part in their own search for change and understanding.

To them and to the therapists who took part we owe a great debt. They have each in their own way demonstrated a deep commitment to each other, and have furnished the reader with a unique opportunity of comparing not only their own approaches, but also the reader's response to the client with their own. (Following the client's original story in Chapter 2, the reader will find space in Chapter 3 to record ideas, questions and feelings with headings that are similar to those questions we asked each therapist.) The therapists have also shown a willingness to work cooperatively in a project which will do much to advance the comparative study of the many different approaches and nuances which the psychotherapy and counselling world embraces. This series shows how little need there is for competition, and how the different therapies can complement one another in the service of those who seek their help.

AN UNWANTED CHILD?

Charlie is medium to tall in height, slightly built and, as the opening words explain, she has long hair, which has a natural curl and care-free quality. She is casually dressed in a denim skirt and white top. Charlie speaks very easily and often quite rapidly, and sometimes follows the track of a story or incident through to a point where she appears to have forgotten where she started. For this reason, in the first interview I occasionally brought her back to 'You were saying . . .' or 'I wonder if you could tell me a little more about . . .', referring back to where she had begun to trail off. It felt as if such interventions were occasionally necessary to save her some embarrassment at having got into a form of expression that had begun to lose substance. There is a nervous quality about her, with a lot of use of her hands as she speaks, and sometimes a somewhat jerky quality to her movement. The most obvious emotion in her is frustration and anger, and several times she raises her voice; she speaks forcefully anyway, but once or twice she actually shouts. She is also just on the edge of tears when she talks about her grandfather's death.

My occasional comments taking her back to an earlier position are omitted. Most of what Charlie said just flowed:

To be honest, last night I was having second thoughts about coming, in case I was wasting your time. When I first thought about therapy, I thought I didn't really have anything that is worthwhile talking about. But a couple of weeks ago my mother 'phoned, and by the end of the 'phone call I was in tears; and she didn't seem to notice, or if she did notice she didn't seem to care. When I put the 'phone down I said, 'Sod it! Where's that leaflet?' Then last night I thought, 'Just talking about my mother, that's a bit feeble, really'.

But ever since I left home, which was partly or mostly because I was unhappy there, I've been trying to do what I wanted to do, and not what my mother wants me to do. A good example of how she controls me indirectly was two weeks ago, when my daughters went to stay with her for a week. While they were there I decided that my hair was getting far too long, and I thought I'd better have it cut. I made an appointment to have it cut and permed. But when they came back last Sunday, they said 'Grandma says you should have your hair cut'. I thought, 'Bloody hell!'; and the next morning I 'phoned up and cancelled the appointment. And I thought [*Charlie shouts*]: 'I am still letting her . . . when I want to make a decision, even a trivial one, I think "What would my mother do?", or I find out what my mother would want and I do the opposite. At my age – I'm forty-two next birthday. I've got three children of my own, the eldest is leaving school next year. I shouldn't be doing that now'.

A lot of what I know about my relationship with my mother I couldn't possibly remember, but I've been told it by my mother herself, and by my grandparents and aunts, and I try not to re-interpret it. She was married at the age of eighteen because she was pregnant, and I was born three months after that. They'd only decided on a boy's name, so clearly they were hoping for a boy. And I was a girl. And my father was on his National Service in Germany when I was born and so she had to think of a girl's name quickly, so she could register my birth, and she had a friend at school called Charlie, who was from a refugee family, so she called me Charlie, and it's been a burden to me ever since. I get letters addressed to '*Mister* C. Bretherton', and it's such a conversation stopper. By the time I've finished explaining how I got my name people have got bored – not surprisingly.

I was born just before my mother's nineteenth birthday. She's always said quite openly that if the 1967 Abortion Act had been the 1947 Act I'd never have been born. In some ways I can sympathize with her. I was twenty-six when I had children, and if I had been pregnant at eighteen it was certainly an option I'd have considered. But if that had happened to me I would want to be honest with that child when the child was old enough to understand; but I would also make it plain that by the time the child was born she was wanted. And she never said that. It was almost as if she was making it plain that they didn't want children anyway, and I should have been a boy, and that when I wasn't that was just it.

Other things that I've been told: like when two and a half I had whooping cough, and I had it quite badly, and I was admitted to hospital for about a week; and my mother said that the doctor told her not to be too hopeful. She says it in a way that she was then quite upset, but almost as soon as I recovered my father became ill with what was supposed to be a mild kidney infection. But it turned out to be polycystic kidneys, and when I was five he died. I was ill for a very long time right through childhood and it's almost as if as I got stronger he got weaker. Almost as if I had in some way caused it.

It's strange, but a similar pattern . . . during my childhood I was quite ill, and it wasn't until I was eleven or twelve that I began to attend school quite regularly, and that was just the time when my grandparents became ill. You can understand that, because they were much older than me, and grandparents do die as children reach adolescence, but *all* of mine seemed to die at the same time as I got noticeably stronger.

And then the same thing happened – a year ago – none of us knew it at the time but to die from his kind of illness at the age of twenty-six is quite rare. My father's mother also died from polycystic kidneys about ten years ago, and then last year my sister was diagnosed as having the same. Mary's three years younger than me. She was born just after my father was taken ill. What she had runs in families, and everyone did investigations into our ancestry. I had to get in touch with my doctor because there was a fair chance I was carrying the same gene. I was a bit worried. Ever since then I've been having tests; and I haven't got it, which means my children haven't got it. But she's got three children too, and they'll all have to be tested when they're older. I was quite pleased, not just for myself, but also for my children because the tests were bloody awful. I didn't want them to go through what I'd been through. But when I 'phoned up my mum to tell her, it was almost as if it was happening again. 'Mary's been ill, she has to have dialysis and is waiting for a kidney transplant. All her children will have to go through it. Charlie's got off scot free yet again, and Mary's the one who is ill'. That quite upset me. My mother said, 'You're lucky again'. I said, 'What do you mean?' She said, 'Well, poor Mary always gets it worse'. Yet when I was ill as a child my mother was always telling me it was all hypochondria: 'Why can't you get out of bed and be strong like your sister?' Now when I am it's as if it's all my fault.

On the other hand, she was a bit ambivalent. Now that I'm older, like just after I had my first child, I had breast abscesses, and I had to go back into hospital, and when I came out she came up and stayed with me for a week, and then she was wonderful – as if when I was weak and helpless that was just how she wanted me to be. When I was a child that's how I was, and all she ever had to do to me was nurse me and look after me, and it seems as if that's the only way she can really relate. I must have done *something*, I suppose.

I don't ever remember being a difficult child, apart from needing constant looking after, but I must have done.

Just after my father died I was sent away to a friend of hers in London. I was a bit upset at the time – any child would be. I do remember crying for a long time, but after that in some ways it was quite pleasant because I liked them. The friends I was staying with, they didn't have any children of their own. The husband was a lorry driver, and he knew London quite well, and at weekends he would take me out to see the sights. Obviously I was too young to appreciate it, but he took me to the top of the Monument, and showed me the view, and told me the story of the Fire; and he took me to the top of the gallery in St Paul's, where you can make [Charlie whispers expressively] a really small noise and it sounds really loud, and you can hear people talking below you. [She sounds very excited as she tells of this.] I remember standing underneath the dome and looking up and it was so *vast*, and when I got up to the top, and you could hear the voices below, and the echoes, oh it was magnificent! I've never forgotten it. I used to think, 'It was a long time ago, maybe I dreamed it'. But I see them occasionally, and I asked them and he said he remembers it vividly. They were really kind people. I went to college in London and I lived not far from them; and I went to see them occasionally and they still took an interest in me. Really nice people.

I picked up a London accent, and after a year when I came home to my mother I cried for my foster parents. While I was there I went to a very traditional old-fashioned infant school, where we all had to sit in rows and wear a uniform. And by the time I came back to Blackburn I was reading, and I went back to my old school and I was streets ahead of anyone else. I was laughed at a bit for my accent, like I was in London when I first went there, but after a bit I picked up my old accent.

When I was ill I used to read a lot, and sometimes when I was well I went to the local library and got some books out. And then I'd be ill and couldn't take the books back, and I'd ask my mum to take my books back. In those days you used to get a postcard saying that if you don't take the books back you get a county court summons. Only then would my mother take my books back, and then I'd have to pay the fine out of my pocket money – yet the library was only a ten-minute walk away. Why wouldn't she take my library books back? It just seems so insensitive.

Another thing that happened: when I sat the eleven-plus, we got the results in the spring on a Friday afternoon, and everybody either had a letter saying you were going to grammar school, or you were going to a secondary modern school. I didn't get a letter at all. I

went up to my teacher and said, 'Everyone's got one. Where's mine?'
He said, 'Ah, there's some problem with yours. You'll get the results
next week'. I went home, and my mother thought it was a bit odd;
and on the Monday we went into school, and went into the head-
master's office. I can remember this extremely vividly, it was a such
a shock really. She said, 'Why hasn't Charlie got her results?' And
he said, 'Well, when the results came I just didn't believe it. So I
rang the department and I asked them to check; and they said the
results they'd got were what I'd got'. And he asked them to go back
and look at all the papers and make sure. My mother said, 'Why?'
And he said, 'Because the results show she'd passed and I didn't
think that was possible'. And I thought, 'He thinks I'm stupid. He
thinks I'm so stupid that he's prepared to stand there [*Charlie is
getting more angry*] in front of me and say that because he thinks I
can't understand it'. [*She raises her voice.*] It sounds really silly now,
but I thought, 'I've read more books than anybody else I know; [*her
voice cracks a little*] I can't be that stupid'.

In some ways it was quite a revelation, firstly that I was thought of
in that way; and also the other thing I suddenly thought of was, 'I
know what he's thinking'. And I hadn't realized before that you could
do that. Obviously every adult knows about interpersonal perception,
and as I grew older I found lots of people could do it, to varying
degrees. But I'd never realized that before. It was the beginning of
a life-long hobby. Because I was an ill, delicate child, I discovered a
long time ago that if you're quiet and sit in a corner with a book
people will talk over your head as if you're not there. Sometimes
you hear things you'd rather not hear. But also you hear a lot, and
if you put it altogether and think about it you can work out what
makes people tick. It all sounds very obvious, of course. But then it
was all new to me. Every time I'm on a train or in a boring meeting
and not saying much, I can look at the other people. So although
it was a very unpleasant experience, a lot of good came out of it.

When I realized afterwards that I knew what he was thinking, I
thought, 'He doesn't know that I knew what he was thinking, but
I know I knew what he was thinking, and so I must be quite bright
really if I could work that out'. And I did pass the eleven-plus. The
main reason he thought I wasn't going to was that I had hardly
been in school more than two or three weeks at a time. It was
around then I began to get stronger and attend school more. But it
was not that good a thing really, because I thought, 'If it was that
easy to pass, then you don't need to work' – I mean, I'd hardly been
at school for a whole term since I started. Once I got to grammar
school I must admit I didn't work as hard as I might have done. But
I got O-levels and A-levels and went to college.

The main reason I stayed on at school was because I thought, 'If I do I can go to college or university, and that's an easy way of leaving home'. I was unhappy at school. It was an achievement, but it wasn't the nicest thing that could have happened. It was a very traditional elitist girls' grammar school. We lived on a council estate, and one of the first things the teachers asked you was which primary school you had come from. If you could say one of the schools in the nice areas you were 'in', and if like me you said 'Elm Street' you were 'council estate' and 'out'. A group of us used to go around together who were known as 'the council estate girls'. It was very rigid, strict discipline, which I found quite hard to cope with. I didn't make the most of it to be honest; but in some ways it was difficult, to make the most of it when it was so . . . I had a funny experience talking about it once on a course – we were told to talk about something, but not too personal. I thought, 'It's over twenty years ago, I'll talk about that'; but after two or three minutes I got really angry [*and Charlie gets angry as she speaks*] – it was really disgraceful what they did to us.

But I was unhappy at home too. In my last year, in the sixth-form, my mother remarried, and the man she married was an absolute bastard, and I couldn't understand why she was marrying him – in fact, she was divorced three years later – except that having been alone for 13 years she wanted someone to live with, I suppose. I can't imagine she didn't have nicer men than that.

He was all right with me, because I was only there for six months after they got married. But I know he did hit my sister, and my mother as well. But he never did that to me. I just didn't like him. I thought he was unpleasant, objectionable and opinionated. He never did anything to me that I could use as an excuse for not liking him. I just didn't like him. I thought all he was after was that she had a house, and he was homeless at the time, and that was what he wanted. I didn't like him. It was a surprise when I came back from my college, and my sister said he was violent. I hadn't ex-pected that.

My mother was very domineering then. Because I was older and stronger and I could do more things, obviously I was going out and meeting other people. Some people say it's an advantage to have children when you're young, because you're still young when they're growing up, but in my experience it's a definite disadvantage, be-cause obviously when I was born I stopped her doing things that older friends did, they were still going out and enjoying themselves. I didn't have children until I was twenty-six, because I wanted to do the things young people like to do, travel a bit, and feel I'd lived a bit myself, before I devoted myself to bringing up children. I was a mistake, and it was one she came to regret quite a lot, because I've heard her say how much she used to envy her friends still going out at night, when she was stuck at home with a child. Most of her friends didn't get married until six years after she did – I was bridesmaid at one of the weddings. She resented that then, but when I was older, and I started doing that, she resented it because I was able to and she hadn't. Also the opportunities were open to me. She had to leave school at fourteen and get a job in an office – I can sympathize with it – I could have left at sixteen if I'd wanted to, but I'd already decided that I wanted to leave home. She used to try and put pressure on me not to. She didn't actually say, 'You can't go out', but she'd say things like, 'Haven't you got any homework to do? Shouldn't you be getting an early night? I think you should only go out on Saturdays'. I do remember having quite vicious rows. Also, she was very suspicious that I might be indulging in sexual behaviour long before I should have done – she was always going on about me, always going on at me, 'It's wrong. You shouldn't do it. You shouldn't have sex before marriage'.

She said that being a woman was an unpleasant thing to be. I remember when I started my periods, it was 'You've got the curse now: you'll find out what it's really all about'. It's not the way I told my own daughter about it. It was always 'women suffer'. I can understand why, because she had. It can't have been easy, having me, in 1950, but she had no choice I suppose. She had to get married and then she was left alone with two young children, and it was a great struggle. By the sixties, when I was in my teens, she was working full-time, and both me and my sister had Saturday jobs, so we weren't as poor as we had been in the fifties. But by then it was always, 'Men only want one thing. It's best to keep away from them. You don't want to stay out. You want to stay at home and study'. And also she would tell me that I wasn't attractive, so if a man did want to go out with me it was only because he was after one thing; it was not because he liked me.

In the sixties, skirts were getting shorter, and when I first came home from town with a short skirt she thought I was tarty. And I shortened all my existing skirts and that was tarty too. The odd thing about my school was that we were actually allowed to wear our skirts short – the only girls' school in Blackburn that were initially. My mum was outraged. I've still got the original skirt that I bought – it was pale blue, and had a big wide belt, and only about three inches above my knee, but I hardly got the chance to wear it, because my mother was so against it.

I haven't thought much about how all this affected me and men. When I went away it was a bit of a shock. I remember sitting in my very first lecture, and there were men in the room. I'd had a few boyfriends – nothing very serious. I regarded men as being very different to women, almost as if they were a different species, if you like. It was a long time before I was able to talk to a man on the assumption that he could understand a lot of what I was saying. It was actually very difficult.

As well as my foster father I did have a very good relationship with my grandfather. He lived not far from us. As a child we all lived there until the housing department split us all up; we all lived within a few streets of my grandmother's house. My mother was one of six children, and she was the youngest but one, so I had a lot of older cousins; and we all used to go to my grandmother's house on a Saturday. My grandfather was very fond of me. He died when I was sixteen. I remember he used to tell me fairy stories that were a bit different from everybody else's fairy stories, although I didn't notice it at the time. He was a very active trade unionist, and he was in the Communist Party for quite a long time, but he told me he resigned over the Hungarian uprising and joined the Labour Party. I know I used to get 'Little Red Riding Hood' as a classic example of socialist mutual self-help: going to her grand-mother's – the wolf was a capitalist obviously [*she laughs*]; and the woodcutter who comes in and rescues everybody was a union mem-ber, and at the sight of his union card the wolf gives up and runs away. And I thought that was what 'Little Red Riding Hood' was, until my sister had a fairy tale book, and I read 'Little Red Riding Hood', but [*she raises her voice in mock protest*] 'That's not the way I heard it!' And Snow White was an exploited woman doing the housework, while the dwarves went off and worked: and that was working-class exploitation as well about the division of labour. Women did housework, and the men worked in the mines. And from a very early age it was dinned into me that once I got a job I would join a trade union; when I was twenty-one, I would vote Labour; and I would have to vote, and I would never even dream of not voting because of what the suffragettes had suffered so that I could have the vote, and what early trade unionists suffered so that working-class people could have the vote. In fact my fifteenth birth-day present was a card; inside it was a postal order for 7/6d (which was the Labour Party subscription in those days), and the Labour Party membership application and [*Charlie raises her voice in emphasis*] this was an honour!

I was more upset when he died than I was . . . I don't remember my father dying at all. Sixteen was quite a bad time – just before I did my O-levels. I remember him saying to my mother, 'Leave the girl alone' whenever she was shouting at me. She used to tell me . . .

like not having my hair cut: I always had to have my hair the way she wanted it, and wear the clothes she wanted, and when I was old enough to buy my own clothes she was obviously very angry that I didn't share her taste. But my grandfather used to say, 'Oh, she looks nice in jeans'.

I think of myself as someone who lacks self-confidence and feels she always has to apologize for herself, and I'm very insecure. The mildest row with my husband and I think he's going to leave me, and he finds that very irritating, I think. Understandably. I would. Having thought about it, I blame her for that. I use the word 'blame' quite consciously, because all the while I very much got the impression when I was young that she didn't love me and doesn't love me. I think of myself as unlovable.

And yet I have friends. I am sometimes very surprised that I do have friends. And that's something else I blame on my mother. For example, one of my friends, perhaps the closest friend I've ever had, is a woman called Barbara – who's a district councillor. I first met her because I'm still in the Labour Party and she was the councillor for the branch I belong to. And I used to really admire and respect her from a very long distance, and look up to her; and after I had known her for a few years, she began to make it quite obvious that she thought well of me and she sought out my company; and that she wanted to be a friend of mine; and I could just not believe it. And I thought, 'A woman like that: what on earth would she see in someone like me? I'm not as intelligent as her, not as decisive as her. She's everything that I would always want to be: she's confident, she's outgoing, she's successful, and yet at the same time like me she brought up a family, and had to combine that with a career, and I'm not just on that level'.

And yet I do have quite a good job, I've brought up three children. I've a son aged fifteen, a daughter aged twelve and another daughter who's eight – she's the little girl I think is most like me when I was a child: quiet, contained, shy, and also a lot happier than I was. So far they are turning out quite well. And my husband tells me that other people talk about me with a fair amount of respect. And I find this unbelievable, because I'm not the sort of person that people like. It causes me problems in that although we are close friends now, she was put off by what appeared to be my dislike of her, which was only really because I could not believe that she could possibly like me.

I may be wrong, and I'm sure I'm to blame myself somewhere along the line, but I feel very strongly that it was my mother that did that to me; that she taught me that I was dislikable, that there was nothing valuable about me, that I'm a worthless person, that

I'm a nuisance to people, that when I'm ill I'm a nuisance; and when I'm not ill I'm difficult, argumentative, tarty, common, and that there is nothing about me that people could possibly like. And although I try very hard not to believe it, I've internalized it to the extent that there's this voice in my head all the time that is telling me, 'It doesn't matter what I do, I will never be a worthwhile person'. And that voice – it's my mother's voice, it's her voice, it's her facial expression, and I still feel controlled by that.

Like in looking after the children. You know the child's constant cry 'It's not fair'. And when you've got three you get it all the time. I do try to be fair. But once I caught myself, I did actually say, 'Life isn't fair, you have to put up with it'. And I thought, 'My mother said that to me once'. And there's probably a fair amount of truth in that, but even so I'll never say that again. And when one of my children wanted to have the pudding first at meal-times, I thought, 'Well, why not? My mother would never allow it'. So for about three or four weeks on Sundays we had the pudding first, until the child got tired of it and we went back to normal meals!

I look back on my life and apart from marrying my husband, which I actually did because I wanted to (I can't say I married him because I knew my mother wouldn't like him, although she doesn't), but everything else I've done just about, is because I've thought to myself, 'What does my mother want me to do? Right, I'll do the opposite!' And that isn't right. You shouldn't behave like that. You should make decisions on what you want, or what you think is the morally right thing to do. You shouldn't let yourself be dominated to that extent. And in reacting to it I'm still allowing her to control me. I resent that. I would like to be autonomous – I suppose is the right word. But I don't think I ever will be now.

Although she's only eighteen years older than me, she still is older than me, and one day she's going to die. And barring accidents I'll still be alive, and I'll be left with all the guilt, because I never tried hard enough to have a good relationship with her. I ought to – she is after all my own mother. She brought me up. She did a lot for me really. I've only talked about the bad things – it can't have been easy for a widow with two children to give me the choice of staying on at school. But she did. Although she did send me away for a year, it was only because she couldn't cope with two children, and I understand that. As soon as she felt able to I was brought back again, and she was absolutely determined that we would stay to-gether as a family, and that I would not be put into formal care. And I don't know – I don't think I could have coped as a single parent with a child of five and another of eighteen months.

The ironic thing is that I did have an abortion, funnily. It wasn't funny at the time, but it's ironic in that she didn't. And that's something else I've benefited from. It makes me feel very guilty actually. It wasn't an abortion like hers would have been. It was ten years ago. It was the tenth anniversary this year – I've just remembered. I'd already got two children. It was a planned pregnancy, but when I was 20 weeks it was diagnosed as deformed, so I was offered the option of either an abortion now, or a still birth, or a child that only lived for a few hours. I thought, 'I've already got two children. I know what a full-term labour is like. The only thing that got me through it before was the thought that at the end of it I shall have a baby. If I have to do that knowing that the baby has to die I don't think I'll cope with it'. So I decided, after talking with my husband, that I would go ahead with the termination. My mother's reaction was quite revealing. It was the only time when I've been in hospital. (She doesn't live in Blackburn anymore. She moved to the coast not long after she married my second stepfather, who's a really nice man – sometimes I wonder why he ever married my mother because he's so much nicer than she is.) But it's the only time she's never come while I was in hospital, to look after my own children or to stay with me after I've come out of hospital. My husband took time off work, he wanted to be with me.

I 'phoned her up, she said she'd call back; and she said, 'It's over now, what you must do now is just forget about it'. And what I wanted more than anything was to talk about it, and she wouldn't let me do that. And I thought, 'This is what she always said she would have done, and now she refuses even to discuss it'. I think actually she was angry with me and thought I was being selfish for having the abortion rather than going on with the pregnancy. But I suppose that was a decision that I did make on my own. I didn't consider my mother at all.

Although there are a lot of issues arising out of that that concern me, I still feel that I made the right decision, for my husband and my children. I could have talked to him – he's a teacher, and he's involved in pastoral care, and has done things like bereavement counselling – but I could only talk to him if he could talk to me, and I couldn't cope with his feelings as well. So I didn't talk to anyone in the end. In retrospect it was a mistake. That's how it goes.

My mother telling me about her wish for an abortion made me feel unwanted. My mother told me that she did sit in a hot bath with a bottle of gin. I quite like gin actually [*she laughs*]. But I must have been fairly determined. Hot baths don't work anyway.

The only way I can cope with her now – I only speak to her on the telephone. If I go and stay with her at all it's only a weekend. The only way I can cope with her now is that I let her talk at me, and I just keep quiet, and agree with everything she says; and I don't cause an argument; I don't cause any trouble, and as soon as I get away from her I think [*deep sigh*], 'I did that really well, I didn't cause any arguments and everything she said was absolute rubbish. I'm bringing up the girls wrong'. We don't have a relationship really. I will feel guilty if it's still the same when she dies. As I said, she's my mother. She may not like me that much, but I feel I *ought* to like her. She didn't have an abortion. She did bring me into the world. She did bring me up. If there is anything worthwhile about me then I must owe some of that to her.

I suppose I feel a lot of guilt about not sharing her priorities. I mean she's very house-proud: her house is always beautiful and very clean; and I'm – to be honest – I'm hopeless. I mean, I keep my kitchen clear and I clean my bathroom and toilet because elementary hygiene says that, but the rest of my house is a bit of a mess; it's not dirty but it's untidy. I don't clean the windows very often, and I look round the house and I think, 'My mother wouldn't like this'; and then I think, 'I'd better get on and clear it up, but I'm not cleaning it up because I want to or because I want my house to look nice, I'm doing it because my internal mother tells me to and makes me feel guilty because I haven't, I suppose'.

I'm a secretary to a senior trade union official and when I'm at work I know I'm good at my job, and I enjoy it, and I feel as if when I'm at work I'm a different person. I'm in control of . . . I run the office, when he's off around the country, as he usually is, I'm in charge, I'm responsible for everything that happens in the office. I have to see that the typing gets done, that the letters get posted. People come in wanting to see him and he's not there. I see them instead. I do a lot of interviewing and welfare rights advice; and I have had to learn a lot about trade union law and social security; and I know when I tell people, 'You are entitled to such and such a benefit', or 'It will be difficult for you to do this or that', that that is the truth, and that I can then go on to advise them of the best way of applying. And I can on their behalf get in touch with authorities. And I know I'm doing a good job and I feel in control of myself, and independent. As soon as I leave the office and I come back home, or I'm seeing other friends, all the while I am regressing back to the little girl that my mother made – would want me to be. It's only when I'm at work that I feel like an adult person.

THE READER'S

RESPONSE

Before reading further, the reader is given space to record a personal response to the client, and to questions similar to those which the six therapists were asked to address.

What does this client make you feel?

How might you use what you feel in understanding and working with this client?

What more do you want to know? Is there any information which is crucial at this stage?

Thus far, how do you understand this client and the material she has presented?

What indications are there so far in this client that lead you to feel that you could work with her?

What contra-indications are there?

What, if any, will be your focus?

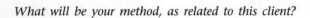

What will be your method, as related to this client?

What difficulties do you anticipate you might encounter?

What in your view might be a favourable outcome for this client?

4

KLEINIAN PSYCHOTHERAPY

The therapist

In 1947, I attended the University of Birmingham and took a then innovative degree in philosophy, economics and psychology (PEP). This course was designed for demobilized soldiers returning to education and was probably a forerunner of the modular degrees now available at every university.

I graduated in 1950 and worked in academic publishing until 1954 when I married, enjoying the role of housewife and mother to my two children, a girl and a boy. In 1956, a close friend persuaded me to apply to the National Marriage Guidance Council (MGC) for training as a counsellor and I stayed at the MGC, eventually as a national tutor, before returning to academic work as a psychology student at Birkbeck College.

I had no idea at the time that the Birkbeck course had such a strong emphasis on scientific models and theories and I was a rebellious student arguing my way throughout the course. I was rescued from my desire to leave the course only by certain tutors who were less antagonistic towards the psychodynamic approach I favoured and who were positive and encouraging towards my struggle with science. I obtained my degree in 1969 and followed this by a special diploma in abnormal psychology. In my final year at Birkbeck, three significant avenues opened before me: (1) I started my personal analysis with a Kleinian analyst; (2) I was accepted at the Tavistock Institute for their course in psychotherapy (for psychologists); and (3) I was offered a job as counsellor/therapist at the University of London Student Health Service.

I worked with my analyst for five years. I look back on these years with gratitude. I learned so much and was fortunate enough at this time also to have the support and facilitation of talented teachers and supervisors.

In the years that followed I did many things. I attended a psycho-analytically orientated group for four years, whose remit was to look specifically at the problems of students in higher education, and I trained at the Institute for Group Analysis and later became a group leader facilitating several kinds of groups, but especially those which focused on supervision and training. I followed this by training in personal construct psychology and looked at a reconciliation of the dynamic Kleinian psychotherapy which I practise and the develop-mental cognitive psychology offered by the Kelly model.

Again I was fortunate to be appointed senior counsellor to the then Harrow School of Technology and Art, witnessing the evolution of the institution into a college of higher education, a polytechnic and then a university, where I am currently both Head of the Harrow Counselling and Advisory Services, and Senior Lecturer and Course Leader for the Harrow Counselling Courses.

When asked to consider the particular value of my Kleinian ori-entation and training in relation to the work I do with my clients, and in this case with a particular client – Charlie – this hinges on the fact that I will have studied my clients in detail and in depth to ascertain their needs and their expectations of therapy. It is usual in therapy to maintain a relationship over many months; and in the process to work through projections and introjections experienced in early childhood relationships, which are of both a positive and negative nature; and to stay with these situations when all too easily they could lead to the abandonment of the therapeutic relationship.

Kleinian psychotherapy focuses in particular on the early years of life and early mother–child experiences which are crucial to the development of the individual from infancy to adulthood. To some it offers a bleak point of view: life is not the proverbial bowl of cherries but a series of unpredictable events thrust upon the indi-vidual, events that have to be experienced, overcome, endured, recon-ciled, call it what you will – but with the hidden agenda and belief in the underlying knowledge that human beings have a unique capacity for endurance.

Further information requested

I asked Charlie the following questions in order to obtain a view of the sequence of events in her life which prompted the question, 'Charlie – An unwanted child?'

What did your mother say over the telephone that caused you such distress and made you move towards therapy?

I know by the end of it I was in tears so she must have said something really painful ... it was about my sister ... and I always seem to say the wrong thing to my mother about my sister. I think she had been asking me about the last DNA I had just had ... which had cleared me completely. I said – it was meant to be sympathetic but I don't think my mother saw it that way – I said the last time I had spoken to Mary [her sister] she had seemed very depressed. I had been asked if I could take part ... there's a new blood test for it, they need some of my DNA ... but they need some of Mary's as a control as well ... I had been asked for my sister's consent and also the name of her doctor but she'd been so depressed when I spoke to her on the 'phone, I thought, 'I won't mention it now, because it just reminds her more really'. My mother got very angry and said, 'You should have done because it's for her own good' ... She was implying that I didn't care about Mary and the way she felt and I didn't sympathize with anyone else except me ... It all came out again, the fact that I was selfish ... I was trying to protest but she wasn't taking any notice. In the end she said, 'I'll call back next week' and put the 'phone down. I got very upset.

Have you thought about what you would like from your therapy? What would you like to happen and what do you feel you need?

I suppose I would like to find out more about myself. Maybe, be able to see myself as others see me, a little bit. I suppose I expect it to be difficult, not necessarily what I want to hear, but I think if I could find out where I'm responsible for how I am, I could perhaps take responsibility for myself.

There's a difference there – do you see what I mean? That's what I would hope for. I hope that's what I would get.

Tell me more please Charlie about how your parents got together in the first place. Where did they meet?

It's embarrassing actually. It's a sort of family legend. My grandparents' wedding anniversary was Boxing Day. On Boxing Day 1949 it was their silver wedding anniversary, which is actually a bit embarrassing in itself because my aunt Beth was born in 1919, so they were obviously not married when she was born. It's a bit difficult when you think about it to be a disgrace to a family like mine ... Everything was

geared to this – the first big celebration since before the
war ... and, according to my mother and to all of her sisters,
my mother had a lot to drink and it was as a result of that
she conceived me. My father was actually on his National
Service at the time; he had come home for Christmas and
that's how I got started. So when people tease me about
being born on 25 September, which is nine months after
Christmas ... according to my mother it was Boxing Day,
and it was all very unfortunate because it was, so she says,
the first time, and she was really unlucky.

*What can you tell me about your grandmother? What kind of a person
was she? Did your mother have a good relationship with her mother?*
In some ways my grandmother was very shadowy in the way
I saw her. She died when I was twelve ... I know my
grandmother was much more upset than my grandfather
when my mother became pregnant with me, and was in fact
very hard on my mother. I don't know in what way, but
that is how she described it. She never talks about my
grandmother now at all and, thinking back, whenever I saw
them together they never appeared particularly close.

*What kind of pregnancy did your mother have? How and where were you
born?*
I should have been born in the maternity hospital, but I was
one of those babies that comes very quickly and I was
actually born in my grandmother's house just before the
ambulance came. I know quite a bit about my birth. It's a
family joke. I gather that because I was her first, she wasn't
really aware of what to expect. She woke up early in the
morning about 6 o'clock with what she thought was
wind ... we had an outside toilet ... and she went down
there and sat for hours on end ... and eventually my
grandmother came down ... and my mum said, 'Yes, I've got
this terrible wind, it sort of coming and going'. My
grandmother immediately panicked, fetched my grandfather
out of bed ... to call an ambulance. By the time the
ambulance came I'd come already; my grandmother ... found
some sheets (not her best sheets) to put on the living room
floor. And then I was taken off to the hospital just to make
sure there wasn't anything wrong with either of us – with
my mother – but we were sent home after about four days
because we were both doing so well.

Was your mother able to breastfeed you?
I don't know. She didn't breastfeed my sister, but I don't
know about me, she never says.

Was your father still serving in Germany when you were born?
Yes.

After your birth where did you and your mother live?
With my grandmother until my father came home . . . I think
it was just around the time of my first birthday. When I was
four we moved up the hill where we got the council house.

When your father left the Army, what happened to you and your family?
How did he earn his living? What do you remember of him and yourself?
He was a bookbinder. He was actually twenty-one when I
was born. When we moved up the hill it was the spring and
my father died in the autumn.
   I remember very little of him actually. I've been told an
awful lot that I'm like him both in looks and mannerisms
and things. I remember like photographs, but there are no
photographs . . . but I remember hardly anything to be
honest.

What was your father's family's reaction to your parents' marriage and
the subsequent arrival of a little girl named Charlie?
They always seemed very fond of me, but my mother said
they were really angry about them having to get married . . .
They felt he'd married beneath him. She was a typist,
whereas his family were craftsmen and that sort of thing.
Bookbinding has always been the elitist trade.

Do you know where this idea of preference for a boy baby came from? Did
Mary's arrival come as a surprise, and was she also expected to be a boy?
I think she [mother] just wanted a boy. She was a bit of a
tomboy herself and boys have a lot more freedom. It was
just what she was hoping she would have.
   There was a big gap between us, three and a half years . . .
She was trying for a baby . . . by the time Mary was actually
born she was happy to accept whatever, because she didn't
want me to be the only one.

Taking into consideration your father's illness, was Mary then a wanted
baby?
I think she was at the time she was born. I think she was
definitely in the way later on, because at the time of her

birth my father started tests to find out what was wrong
with him ... when Mary was six months old my mother was
told that his condition was terminal. She was eighteen
months old when he died. My grandmother used to come
and take Mary away for weeks on end ... I was less
trouble ... being able to wash and dress myself.

*I am still not sure why you were sent to stay with the family in London.
You imply that in the early years your mother had little support, but with
five aunts uncles and grandparents ... why were they not involved in
helping to look after you?*
I've often wondered that too, but all my aunts and uncles
had children of their own. My mother had met May [her
friend] at school. She offered to take me ... it was felt that
if I had to go away from home it would be better for me
to get right away, rather than have me somewhere close
by where I would – where it would be easy for me to run
away.

Did you really understand why you were there (in London)?
I'm not sure if I've been told this since or whether I was told
at the time, but I certainly have a clear understanding that
my mother was greatly upset by my father's death ... she
couldn't really cope with two young children. I was the
eldest and I'd been sent to London to be looked after.
   I was very unhappy to begin with – crying to come home
almost all the time – but when I came home to Blackburn I
cried to go back to London ... because I was so attached to
them. It was like being taken away from my mother again.
Looking back on it now, yes, it was one of the happiest
times of my life.

*Was it really better – as you say – to remain weak and helpless in order
to gain the attention of your mother?*
Did I say that? ... Perhaps what they are referring to is that
I've found when I am ill, like just after the birth of babies
and things, my mother comes across and looks after me and
then is marvellous. Yes, it's as if when I am weak and unable
to upset her by being awkward or whatever it is, that's the
way she can relate to me best. I don't know whether I do it
deliberately, but no – I don't become ill deliberately ... I
suppose it's true ... but it doesn't help because it's very
much then a mother–child relationship and I would rather –
I mean – I'll always be her daughter and she'll always be my

mother, but I don't want to be her child, not now I'm an adult, if you see what I mean.

After last time [previous interview] I thought about it . . . and I don't remember being ill [in London] and that surprised me and I did begin to wonder if there might be something in it.

And does she seem to look after Mary?
Yes, I suppose she does. She's very concerned about Mary. Whenever she rings me up, we always get round to Mary eventually.

What about the eleven-plus examination – it seems as though you can experience yourself as powerful – would you agree?
It's probably quite true actually . . . I had more freedom at school . . . in the way I felt about myself . . . I did make connections: 'Yes, you can see what other people are thinking . . .'. A lot of people can do that, but it was the first time it had happened to me. I thought I'm not stupid really . . . I can do things if I want to do them. Even at my grammar school I still used to think, 'I know what other people are thinking, they don't know what I'm thinking and inside my head I can do whatever I want'.

When you get angry about being one of the 'council estate girls', your anger seems quite positive?
That's true actually. It was in the 1960s. A working-class background was . . . trendy. Yes it did make me angry and I was quite consciously . . . a bit rebellious if you like. I deliberately identified myself with that as a way of getting back at some of the snobbishness. A bit over the top to be honest . . .

Always in relation to your mother you say you feel frustrated. Outside you seem to manage quite well but on the inside – when you were developing as a sexually aware young woman – she remained a powerful influence in your life. How do you think she still influences you?
She's very much still there inside my head. Doing that diary [for Anthony Ryle] made me aware of it . . . But externally she still does try. She's forever giving me advice . . . she will tell me what I ought to say . . . word for word. If I had problems with my poll tax or whatever . . . my mother would assume that I couldn't and would tell me who I must see, what I must say, what my job is, how many children I've

got . . . when I'm with the children whatever I do I know it's wrong. I'm either being soft with them or else I'm trying to influence them too much or I'm over-indulging them. It's all tied to being a wonderful mother. She varies a lot in her attitude to my husband . . . he's a lazy slob, she can't see what I saw in him, at other times he's too good for me . . . She tries to interfere between me and my husband quite consciously. Sometimes Andrew says something and I think, 'Don't let my mum hear that'. She wouldn't like it.

But why would she want to inhibit you sexually, tell you that you are unattractive, dislikable, frighten you about menstruation and childbirth, make you feel a nuisance? Why you?
I suppose it was the circumstances of my own conception. She very clearly . . . and I clearly felt and from other people in the family, it was a very difficult time for her. I don't think I was ever to blame for it . . . but as I grew up and developed sexually I reminded her of it. I suppose she didn't want me to have the same problems . . . instead of framing it in that way she tried to put me off any contact with men.
    When I was eighteen, she married my first stepfather – an absolute brute. When I was living at home I didn't have any kind of . . . it was at college that I had my first real relationship which ended unhappily. It was a passionate relationship and this was going on at the same time as my mother was going through a very physically violent experience. By the time I left college, she was getting a divorce. I would talk about Phil, my friend, and the way I felt about him. I suppose the contrast made her more bitter.

Is it just with you, or can you see her behaving in the same way with others – your children for instance?
She never seemed to do it to my sister, and she doesn't seem to do it to my daughters now that they are growing up.

How did you come together with your husband? Tell me more about your relationship with him?
We were both in the Labour Party [*laughs*] . . . I knew him for a year before we got together. I was sharing a flat with Penny, whom I'd been at school with. She was very attractive. My husband quite liked her and kept coming round – she wasn't interested in him . . . she moved to London . . . he kept coming round because he'd got into the

habit of it . . . so he was forced to talk to me. I was looking for someone to share the flat with . . . someone moved in for two weeks over Christmas. Andrew had lent his keys to someone else so he could not get back into his own flat and there was nobody there to let him in, so he thought 'I'll go and see if Charlie's in'. I was struggling to clean up. He made a really good job of helping me. They had moved the furniture about and so in moving it back again I got a splinter in my hand . . . I asked him to take it out . . . I thought he'd be hacking and stabbing at it, but he did it so gently, and I thought, 'Well, he's really nice'. And he ended up staying the night.

You say your mother does not approve of him? Why is this?
He's too much like me . . . she calls us ageing hippies. He's even more untidy than I am. If we're given the choice between reading a book or clearing the bathroom, well then we read a book. I did a general degree which included psychology. He did a psychology degree. He's got all those sort of Carl Rogers type attitudes about unconditional love and he's critical of my mother . . . He thinks we are doing a better job than she did and that our children are growing up a lot happier and more confident than I did.

She liked him originally. Now she thinks he's lazy. I think it's a bit strange, but she taught me to do painting and decorating because she had to do it for herself . . . I'm quite happy to do it on my own, it's my choice. For her having a nice house is the ultimate . . . I've got different priorities. I must admit, yes I am lazy. It's my besetting sin for as long as I remember [*laughs*], it makes me so depressed . . . well depressed is the wrong word but I just get angry with myself.

What after all was your own experience of love?
Phil was on the same course as me . . . He . . . one thing I'd never had before. We shared a lot of the same things, we both liked poetry, Shakespeare. We liked Beethoven and Mozart and rock music . . . Bob Dylan and the Rolling Stones and the Beatles. He was very perceptive. I shouldn't talk of him as if he were dead! I still see him occasionally. I'd catch him looking at me and he'd catch me looking at him. And you'd think, 'He's doing it to me NOW! This is not on, I'm the one who does that, not anybody else'.

He was my first physical lover. *On reading the transcript of this interview through, Charlie sent Michael Jacobs the following*

information in a letter: I was not entirely truthful in one thing
I said. I said that Phil was my first experience of sex and this
is not true. I am sorry about this. I was conscious of it even
as I said it, and I don't know why I didn't correct it straight
away; I will try to make up for it now. This is the way it
really was. I had a few boyfriends before I went to college,
and although I wasn't seriously involved with any of them, I
suppose I wanted to find out what all the fuss was about,
whether I was missing out on something. So I had some
sexual experiences before I met Phil. I was honest about it
being less than overwhelming, and it is also true that I was
frightened of sleeping with Phil and didn't do so for some
time – I wanted it to be different this time, and I was scared
that it wouldn't be. In the event, it was just as bad as before,
at first, and then it was some time before it got better. I've
always believed that the fact that both of us wanted to try
bears witness to the commitment we had to each other. I was
a bit nervous of sex . . . I kept saying 'NO' when I really
wanted to say 'YES'. I was scared. To begin with it was
painful and a disappointment . . . but with practice it got . . .
and then it was wonderful. For three years . . . once a year
we'd have a dramatic row and then we got back together
again. I look back on it now as 'The Golden Age': reading
the books I wanted to read anyway, getting a grant for it,
psychology and ethics, and then Phil on top of that. The
London cinemas and the theatres. It's hard to describe now
because it did finish unpleasantly at the end and led onto
my first sort of really tremendous depression. I had spells of,
I suppose melancholy is the right word, before then. But
those first few months back in Blackburn, I thought I was
going mad.

And marriage?
We drifted into living together, then we got pressure,
particularly from my husband's parents . . . if we legitimized
the relationship. We kept resisting this to begin with, then
somebody mentioned wedding presents and we hadn't got
sheets or anything. Then I found out about if you got
married you got massive rebates. We had both started to
work you know . . . so we said, 'why not then? It might be
fun'. Most of the time it *has* been . . . times when we were
both out of work and I've been pregnant and we've been
really poor. I never came close to walking out. Well if he
has, he didn't say.

And childbirth?
They were all different. I'm not very good at being pregnant.
I get sick at the beginning and get fat and heavy at the end;
in the middle I just get heartburn and bad-tempered.
    The onset of labour pains . . . 'Oh good it's about to finish'.
A few hours later, 'God it's awful'. With James they gave me
an awful lot of pethidine, with Rosalind natural childbirth
was the in thing to do. With Alanna I had an epidural. . . .
no I don't like those people who go around frightening
young women by saying it's absolutely awful. It was never
that bad . . . and the end result was wonderful.

*The many positive things listed – marriage, children, friendships, work –
are all your own achievements. Why do you feel you owe 'anything
worthwhile' about yourself to your mother's influence?*
I suppose I feel that after all she brought me up. From the
age of five she brought me up by herself. Did I say that
'Whatever was worthwhile in me I owe to my mother?' I feel
that I ought. She did many things for me that she didn't
have to do: she let me stay on at school when others in the
family felt that I ought to be out earning money. She let
me . . . encouraged me to go to college. I'm a bit ambivalent
about that because she seemed very pleased to be rid of me!
But again that's what I wanted too, and she did teach me a
lot of independence and self-reliance . . . I suppose I feel I
owe that to her. That makes it worse in a way. I feel I ought
to love her, she's my mother. But I can't. When you listed
the things I achieved, I suppose that must have come from
me, but I don't see them as achievements, I just see it as I've
been lucky really.

Assessment

Most therapists tend to see diagnosis as a separate process from
treatment, but we all have the experience of having seen our patients once or even twice, only to be told afterwards that whatever
happens in that short space of time has had a sufficient impact on
the person and helped them to resolve some of the basic developmental problems in their life.
    Charlie's reaction to her initial interview and the subsequent
questions that are asked of her and her responses illustrate the point
that if personal development is to be made in psychotherapy, a
salient feature is that development does not occur in isolation but

always in relation to persons or objects both internal and external, and that it is the real relationship between therapist and patient which is of fundamental importance.

Charlie's experiences in life are unique to her. She shares with us a primary separation anxiety, which results from the loss of closeness to her mother and the death of two male figures in her life – her father and grandfather.

Charlie's feelings of anxiety are exacerbated when her mother – perhaps even for the most logical of reasons – chooses to send her away in the period following her father's illness and death. A child being sent away from home for whatever reason cannot understand why, and will experience the separation as a form of punishment. Charlie confirms these deepest suspicions. She laughingly suggests that in sending her to college later on, her mother 'got rid of her'. Reassurance is inadequate for Charlie; the fantasized feelings of possible abandonment and rejection, which are latent in all of us, are made a reality.

In Kleinian theory, the earliest state of mind of the child is described as the paranoid-schizoid position. It looks at the ways in which an infant's relationship with both internal and external realities are taken over by the defence mechanisms of splitting and projection. The child's life is full of fantasies, and the child experiences itself as one with the mother, and has feelings of power and omnipotence in which it imagines that it can control the mother – take over the mother, project itself into being at one with the mother. The child cannot imagine or understand the meaning of separateness and seeks to retain control by living inside the mother.

The passage to adult perceptiveness and sensitivity later on in life involves acceptance of the separateness of the self from the mother. This is termed the 'depressive position', a situation in which the child is able to give up its illusions of power and control and accept ambivalent feelings of love and hate for the mother. Accepting such a stark reality brings with it feelings of depression and sadness, and a sense of loss and guilt for what was and what can never be again.

In her first interview, Charlie reveals helpless and frustrated feelings that she might have been concealing from herself and others – a sad and angry child-like part of herself that had not yet grown up and still wanted to be looked after. Instead, she has to be the 'grown-up' girl, who can manage other people's lives and is now also the mother of three children. But she herself had no father and little real mothering since the age of four.

Charlie is bewildered by the conflict of emotions that she experiences with her mother, who is either very good to her when she is ill or in need of help, or very bad to her when she asserts herself as a separate person. During the depressive position, the whole relationship with her mother is undergoing significant changes that are important for her continued development. The good satisfying mother and the bad frustrating mother are one and the same person. At times also, Charlie can experience her mother as a whole person on whom she can depend.

When Charlie becomes angry and frustrated after the 'phone call from her mother, and on the many occasions when she is attempting to communicate her feelings about her sister, Mary, she is afraid of going too far in her anger, afraid of destroying and losing the ties with her mother.

Feelings of anxiety which are aroused after every angry interchange leave Charlie feeling depressed. Charlie also feels guilty and worries about harming her mother, especially when she is able to reflect on the story of her birth, her father's death and her mother's subsequent hardship and poverty. She wants to make things better, to make reparation, to develop the capacity to love her mother, even though she clearly tells me that she does not love her.

In addition, I am aware of the sadistic, envious feelings which Charlie exhibits towards her sister Mary. Melanie Klein emphasized the importance of these feelings in the relationship of the child to its parents. Later she deepened and widened her original concept of envy as the primary source of aggression directed initially against the mother, to stress that aggressive envy in the child is capable of interfering in the development of good and satisfying object relations, and may also severely inhibit the ability to love. The capacity to love is always linked to the capacity to feel compassion and gratitude.

We now know that the concept of envy has significant theoretical and clinical implications, in that it highlights the child's state of confusion and helps us to understand the nature of splitting (the good and the bad). Excessive envy interferes in the therapeutic process. Primary envy is one of the main causes of negative therapeutic reaction. This can be seen in Charlie's situation when, after a period of positive insights into her situation, she may well relapse. The concept of envy remains controversial, even though the identification and confrontation of envy in the patient may well make unconscious guilt accessible, thus facilitating the move towards the depressive position.

The merging of love and hatred in our relationships with significant others in our life gives rise to feelings of uncertainty and sadness. This so-called depressive anxiety fills us with guilt about the ambivalent feelings we experience, particularly about those who are close to us. But as Charlie demonstrates, these depressive feelings are crucial in the development of the adult personality. Without them we could not feel generosity and kindness as well as anger and hatred. In our efforts to maximize the loving aspects of our relationships, we come as close as we can to mobilize altruism and reparation.

Envy can happen wilfully, when during the course of development a child feels angry, upset and displeased, and responds by attacking whatever has or seems to have caused hurt or threat to their existence. The resultant rage and frustration is as likely to be directed at self (Charlie's asthma attacks) as it is at others present in one's environment – mother, father, sister, etc.

While malicious aggression can be identified as the active component in envy, not all anger and aggression is malicious. Demanding and forceful behaviour can be both constructively self-assertive and developmental, and destructive to oneself or others. We have to examine the motivation which stimulates the feeling. The essential components of envy are despair at others' advantages, spiteful rage and destructive behaviour, which produce little material gain or any real advantage over that which is envied:

> Many individuals hate the sense of needing or depending upon another and will do all they can to subvert or destroy dependency. By dependency I mean an appreciation of need, the taking of food and gratitude for being fed.
>
> No one can avoid being dependent but at some point everyone tries to begrudge the experience because dependency involves an awareness of love–hate, guilt, loss and grief. The dependent person attacks these painful feelings in oneself by blaming others. The resulting onslaughts range from a transient grumpiness in the presence of a parent (or spouse or anyone who has or might be trying to provide something) to a defiant negativity.
>
> (Berke 1989: 89)

Therapeutic possibilities

The question I have had to ask myself in relation to Charlie is not whether I am dealing with either a neurotic symptom or a developmental and character problem, but rather how the symptom of abnormal behaviour (if any) is to be understood in the context of her life story and the social environment in which she now lives. For me, such understanding can only be arrived at after a full investigation in face-to-face interviews with Charlie which look at the dynamics which she presents and of her interpersonal relationships.

In the light of such interviews, taking into consideration such factors as our mutual feelings of rapport or discomfort, and some understanding of the transference and counter-transference situation, I could make an initial diagnosis. Together with Charlie I would decide whether she can best be helped by a limited form of treatment, directed mainly at the symptom itself (her need to separate from her mother and to re-connect herself with her father), or whether Charlie is really motivated and capable of working with me at a deeper level, in an attempt to help her get beyond early constraints in her personal development.

The basic assessment on which my decision to work with Charlie would be based must include her ability to understand the unconscious processes involved in therapy. Here Charlie shows glimpses of her insightfulness and ability to accept unconscious motivation when she talks initially of her expectations of therapy: 'I suppose I would like to find out more about myself . . . to see myself as other people see me . . . not necessarily what I want to hear . . . I think if I could find out where I am responsible for how I am, I could perhaps take responsibility for myself'. Reason enough.

On such a basis alone I could make the decision as to whether what brings Charlie to a psychotherapist can best be dealt with by a combination of both my therapeutic function directed towards the relief of her symptoms (feelings of rejection), and the developmental function of therapy, which would be aimed at facilitating her personal growth and development (being her own person).

In working with Charlie, my function would need to be addressed under three separate headings: psychodynamic understanding, therapeutic function and developmental function. I need to understand Charlie in order to arrive at a rational decision of how to help her. To do so I must be able to assess her as a whole person, taking notice of her psychosocial behaviour, her appearance, her sense of timing and commitment to therapy. I need to know more about her conscious and unconscious conflicts, her present life situation as a wife and a mother (barely touched upon in the written presentations), in other words her human relationships. I need to observe Charlie, to look into her face, to maintain the correct balance between doing to and being with. Doing to, writing to, is a form of behaviour which strikes me as implying separateness – a gulf between Charlie and me. The question and answer method we have used tends to isolate areas of Charlie's experience, fragments more likely to be concerned with her outward behaviour than her inner meanings. The 'doing to' function is never enough for me and is not, I suspect, enough for Charlie.

The 'being with' function in therapy demands a high degree of empathy and sensitivity to what Charlie is experiencing – how can

I tell? I need to think carefully, maybe intuitively, to understand the deeper meaning of Charlie's verbal – but even more importantly her non-verbal – responses. How can I do this? What does it mean when Charlie stays silent, when she weeps, goes to sleep, becomes irritated and restless, gets angry and acts out with her body rather than words?

I need to have Charlie there as a person so that she is aware (or doubts) my reliability and genuine concern. When faced with a series of questions and answers, how can Charlie and I refrain from conjecture or from making interpretations which are invalid? How do I avoid becoming embroiled in the identification of symptoms when being with Charlie as a real person is felt to be more important for both of us?

Charlie may well need to re-experience in therapy those early phases of her childhood in which some disturbance has occurred. It is my task to provide her with the conditions which are safe enough to allow her to regress and to make up for earlier damage, thus facilitating a new beginning in her development. This task would make special demands on Charlie, as indeed it also would on any therapist who saw this method as a way of achieving lasting changes in the way Charlie sees her future as well as her past.

The course of therapy

In the interview with Michael Jacobs, Charlie is at first polite and fairly impersonal. Only the rise and fall of her voice provide any real clues to her innermost feelings. Charlie relates her story. She was originally an illegitimate child, her mother was shamed by her pregnancy. She was conceived in a period of drunkenness following a family party. Her mother eventually marries Charlie's father, a young man doomed from birth by a dreadful and terminal illness. The family struggle in poverty; another child, Mary, is born, also carrying in her blood the seeds of her father's terminal illness. Charlie's father dies when she is four years old, but there is little she can remember of him – nothing to hold on to, 'like a series of photographs' flat and faded.

There is a hysterical reaction from her mother. Charlie is sent away from home and brought up in London. Charlie's reactions at home have previously manifested themselves as asthma attacks. Sent to live in the London smog, the asthma attacks disappear. When Charlie returns home there is little joy in her relationship with her mother and she barely mentions her younger sister who remained at home during her absence.

Charlie's subsequent academic success produces surprise rather than accolades from her family, and her only friend and confidant is her socialist grandfather who continues the political views of her dead father and gives her the stimulation and appreciation she needs. Too soon Charlie's grandfather dies, leaving her doubly bereft of the two men in her life.

Charlie succeeds in making me ask her many questions, but it is still hard to get anything like a real picture of her present life situation and past development. There are enormous gaps and I begin to feel doubtful as to whether or how, following this written formula, I could really help her.

I find myself picking up feelings – feelings I share with Charlie – feelings that she might have. Helpless and frustrated feelings that she has been concealing from herself and others beneath her apparently successful image of wife, mother, student.

I wonder whether it is really true, as Charlie has told us, that she had not missed her father when she was a child, and had been content to live with an on-and-off relationship with her mother in the years following his death. Perhaps Charlie found it a greater strain than she liked to admit to have her mother lean on her, and use her as a confidante, since she was a small girl.

I could make this tentative interpretation were I with Charlie. Perhaps then a picture would emerge of the child still within herself, a child who has been carefully concealed from everyone – mother, husband, friends included. Indeed, these are two frightened little children, confronted by their father's death. Charlie has to be 'grown up' and able to function. Did they cry, howl, scream? I would want to know or even to hear.

In later years, Charlie is expected to be a good and helpful daughter, unable to express anger about her mother's possessiveness and demands on her, instead of letting her behave as a child and later on as an independent sexual woman. She cannot express anger because she might be sent away again.

Melanie Klein explains that when a mother hinders or arrests her daughter's sexual activity (as with Charlie), the mother is actually fulfilling a normal function whose lines are laid down by events in her own childhood (the unmarried mother). These powerful unconscious motives to restrict the child receive the sanctions of society even today. It is the task of the daughter to emancipate herself from this influence and to decide for herself on broad and rational grounds what her share of enjoyment or denial of sexual pleasure shall be. Charlie felt inhibited when talking about her early sexual experiences, but was able to understand her mother's envy and frustration when Charlie decided to tell her mother about her relationship with Phil.

However, where the facilitated woman can rest in her family, can leave her childhood home to make another family, the restricted woman can neither leave nor stay. Normal feminine growth and development would have enabled Charlie to make the transference of Oedipal father-love to husband-love. This growth was impeded by the death of Charlie's father and she has not yet been able to make the transition from her family of origin to a family of orientation. If this could be renegotiated successfully, even at this late stage as she the daughter becomes a mother, her ties with her own mother, whose image she confirms, could be strengthened.

Such a radical failure of development, as the aftermath of the death of Charlie's father implies, can be addressed in therapy in that her father is not completely barred access in her mind. She can still accept the place and function of her father, however brief the relationship. In particular, the reality of her parents' sexuality is partially accepted (the drunken intercourse and later the wanted and tried-for baby Mary), but it has been de-emphasized, put back, too shadowy and painful to be acknowledged.

The father's paternal function has been missing from Charlie's early development – there are times when she may unconsciously seek this out (her helpful husband) at the same time as she unconsciously tries to avoid it ('I don't need him to help me').

> A frequent contributor to this situation may be the attitude of the mother who denigrates the role of the father and discourages the child from developing an affectionate relationship with him. This may be an expression of the mother's phantasy that she created the child all by herself. If the father has not been allowed his full place in the mother's mind it may be more difficult for him to find a place in the child's mind – and in this way the disturbance may be transmitted through the generations.
>
> (Mollon 1993: 120)

Problem areas

The essential ingredient in this form of limited therapy is to convey to Charlie that this must be a short-term procedure. First, it has a limited aim, which I hope Charlie is helped to clearly understand. Second, I have to keep this aim in mind when using selective questioning which either draws attention to or completely leaves to one side some of the material which Charlie has provided. This implies an active mode rather than the passive mode I usually employ.

I have had to work blindly (and quickly) to establish through my questioning some measure of warmth, compassion and equality. I have had to base my assessment of Charlie's psychological condition on her written responses, to get an idea of what she is like and what she would like to be like. I feel constricted in that I rate my success as a therapist when I am able to establish a successful personal interaction with my patient.

When conducting these interviews as a conversation, it is so easy to substitute my views for Charlie's and to interrupt with questions in an attempt to relieve her anxiety and my own. In this form of limited therapy, it may well be that Charlie is given more insights that she can utilize at this moment in time. I hope she can eventually make use of it. Brief work of this kind attracts more of the childishness and inadequacy than is experienced in long-term work. I am conscious that it is both dangerous and ineffectual to interpret unconscious material if it is not going to be used in later work. All I can admit to myself and to Charlie is that Charlie makes me feel in a certain way.

As a psychotherapist trained in the Kleinian mode, I am convinced that the transference is present from the very beginning of therapy. This is used, as explained earlier, to investigate not only positive feelings directed towards me by my patients, but negative feelings as well. I can examine my own feelings about Charlie but I have no idea how Charlie is feeling about me. Making this connection is invaluable and I feel its loss.

In working with the transference, Charlie would have an opportunity to examine her expectations and reactions to me – a person who, though sensitive to her story, is not involved in its components. She could then see for herself how easy it is to fall into certain ways of experiencing other people in her life. She may come to conclusions about them that impede her relationships with them. Reasons for these inappropriate assumptions could be understood as Charlie sees them operating in different areas of her life. For instance, if – over a period of time – Charlie could see that her resentment of her sister's relationship to her mother is but one part of the envy she feels for her mother, of her mother's capacity to survive the difficulties in her life, she may then be able to verbalize her envy of me as a therapist for having a specialized training and a (fantasized) 'easier' and more comfortable lifestyle.

If I had the time and the space to work with Charlie, we could look at her ambivalence, her efforts to overcome the guilt she feels as she tries to please her mother and others.

With time and space again, we could examine the limits of her hate and love, giving up Charlie's belief that she can put things right on her own. As a patient, Charlie could acknowledge her need of help and abandon to some degree her insistence on providing for herself. She could tolerate the feelings of depression attendant in realizing that things are not as they could have been if she had not wasted her time and talent in competing with her sister Mary for the attentions of her mother, and in dwelling upon some of the unpleasant aspects of her own personality. As a consequence, Charlie feels robbed of her creativity and productivity. Her life in general has suffered, in particular her work, her sexuality and her social behaviour.

The problem areas in Charlie's story which I would wish to address are:

1 The 'wasting' of her actual birth. The drunken conception, the scene in the toilet with her mother, attempting to evacuate her foetus as wind.
2 The 'second' best sheet used in her delivery and the mess that was made on the living room floor.
3 Little mention of Charlie's own sexual needs and wants as she grew into womanhood; and then the censoring of her sexual relationship before Phil (which Charlie amends, and this is a positive indication for therapy).
4 No real contention with the mourning process and her mother's obvious collusion in construing her father's brief life and his input into the family as 'phantomlike'.
5 The birth of Mary portrayed by her mother (?) as a joy – a cure for emptiness and despair over the diseased body of her father.
6 Later her own mothering is barely touched upon in her account. Joseph Berke described the feelings of one of his male patients thus:

> I was delighted when my son was born. Yet when I held him in my arms for the first time I was seized with a sudden overpowering desire to smash his little body on the ground and stamp on it. This thought made me terribly upset. Then I realized how envious I felt towards the baby. All he had to do was open his mouth and he was fed. I had to work damn hard. His whole life lay before him. Much of mine was past. He had a father who loved him. My dad died years before.
>
> (Berke 1989: 162)

Criteria for successful outcome

Every school of psychoanalysis prescribes a deliberate set of techniques and procedures which tend to glamorize its practitioners. But regardless of the school to which a therapist belongs, Charlie could expect to be free of excessive anxiety and free to make her way towards personal growth and maturation unhampered by her feelings of envy, jealousy and discomfort. I would hope that Charlie could become ready for creative expansion and for self-realization and be able to accept love and tenderness.

Yet in this particular way of working, I have no alternative but to abandon the idea of therapeutic perfectionism and settle instead for a limited goal for her therapy – that of guiding Charlie through a selection of the material she presents. I can, however, decide which problems are not relevant to the progress of her therapy using the following criteria:

- while retaining the details of Charlie's original presentation, relating the features of each incident and classifying them into what is and what is not a problem;
- recognizing the limits of the therapy and discussing this with Charlie;
- observing what has been omitted;
- reinforcing her coping elements and her self-understanding;
- endeavouring to maintain a feeling capacity and not being seduced into intellectualizing.

I remember being told many years ago that D.M. Malan was of the opinion that psychotherapists should attempt to free themselves from the rigidity in believing that anything other than long-term psychotherapy would always be second best. He maintained that he could undertake short-term work with patients as long as they were willing and able to explore their feelings and they were judged to be capable of working within a therapeutic relationship based on interpretation. He wanted to be sure that the therapist was able to formulate some kind of circumscribed therapeutic plan, including the important issue of grief and anger at the termination of therapy.

Later on, the essence of Malan's work was much discussed among psychotherapists, who concluded that the outcome of such therapy could only be successful when there was a willingness on behalf of both patient and therapist to become deeply involved in order to bear the tension that was bound to ensue from short-term work. Inevitably, I feel that I have failed, since I am unable to be with Charlie in the right way at the right time. I want to acknowledge this to Charlie. I am not able to be maternal or paternal enough. I am not able to understand Charlie, since I cannot respond as to whether her demands are reasonable or impossible. I cannot express my anger to Charlie or indeed to allow her to be angry with me – an intrinsic part of Kleinian therapy. Without Charlie's expressed anger towards me, there can be no reparation. And Charlie is angry, very angry, with so many people in her life. This failure must be acknowledged by us both.

These are all ways of genuinely being with her, but they need then to be followed by some form of interpretation, that is by the 'doing to' which comes after the 'being with'. In this way and in this way only could Charlie really begin to experience and recognize the good and bad aspects of herself and of me. This experience needs to be repeated again and again, so that gradually Charlie can accept the bad and the good in herself and in her mother, thereby reducing the primitive splitting which is a basic problem in every human encounter. It is particularly so for Charlie, who got stuck in those early stages of development where splitting is the only model of object relating: You love me – you don't love me.

Summary

Many children and adults act in strangely convoluted ways, not just to disguise their feelings of enmity and rivalry, but to avoid the hatred and the accusations of unfairness that being the loved one may attract. In Charlie's case, there was in her early life a particular absence or intrusion, in fact an extended series of absences and intrusions which she was not really able to bear. Children learn very quickly to brush off hurts, but there are some children who store away hurts and take them out again and again to re-experience them. These children are immune to the usual family patterns of making things better by kissing and making up. If Charlie's mother had been more sensitive to the feelings of a child sent away from home, she could have responded more positively. She did not. And so it was for Charlie that as the years went by trivial deeds became terrible misdeeds and compounded the hurt and pain.

Her reaction was to turn her mother and her sister into persecutors, the focus of angry exchanges and deep disappointments which continue in her life even to this day, and render ineffectual any form of compensation which she could receive from the love of her own children.

She lives in fear of humiliation and ridicule from her mother, and suffers guilt for the many subtle ways she herself uses to run down her mother, her sister and other members of her family. In later life, Charlie has assumed an air of intellectual superiority (the 'right' newspapers left on the floor), yet despite this façade she remains full of enmity and jealousy.

One further aspect concerns the ending of this story. What is to become of Charlie? Where do we go from here? What about the ending of our relationship, constrained as it may be? Do we consider, when the desired results of the exercise have been achieved, what we have done to Charlie, and whether we have given her what she needed as we now discharge her? It is important not to dismiss Charlie but to continue to remain with her as it were. Will I survive in Charlie's mind as a significant inner object or memory? I believe that it is most important for Charlie to know that I continue to exist.

This is not a form of wanting to remain possessively in touch with her, or doubting that she is able to lead a free and independent life. Rather, I want her to know that should she wish to communicate with me, I will be pleased to hear from her. It is a better ending than to write Charlie off. A note of finality is not truly in the spirit of this relationship, which, however ephemeral and transient, I hope can have some meaning for her.

The process of therapy is one of bridging the lonely inner self and the outer world through the therapeutic relationship; I trust even this relationship will help Charlie to continue her psychic experience.

Further reading

Berke, J.H. (1989). *The Tyranny of Malice*. London: Simon and Schuster.
Hinshelwood, R.D. (1994). *Clinical Klein*. London: Free Association Books.
Klein, M. (1960). *Our Adult World and Its Roots in Infancy*. London: Tavistock.
Mollon, P. (1993). *The Fragile Self*. London: Whurr Publishers.

PHIL LAPWORTH

5 TRANSACTIONAL ANALYSIS

The therapist

I started out as a teacher in special education. Over the years, particularly in my post at a psychiatric hospital school and later at a day-school for children with learning difficulties, I was introduced to behavioural, psychodynamic and humanistic approaches to helping troubled children and adolescents. Wanting to learn more, I took a three-year course in counselling skills. This was a broad-based, self-directed course encompassing several approaches to counselling: person-centred, gestalt, psychodynamic, transactional analysis and re-evaluation counselling. I focused more on working with adults and, after fifteen years in the field of education, I set up as a counsellor in private practice, gained accreditation with the British Association for Counselling and began my psychotherapy training.

From these divergent and eclectic introductions to various approaches, I became more convergent in my development by training as a transactional analyst. I found transactional analysis (TA) clarifying and illuminating in its theoretical constructs, simple yet profound, certainly not simplistic (though, unfortunately, I think it is sometimes misused in this way) and capable of integrating much from behavioural, psychodynamic and humanistic theories and approaches.

After qualifying as a clinical transactional analyst, I diverged again by taking a course in systemic integrative psychotherapy designed for qualified psychotherapists from diverse theoretical backgrounds. Here again was a widening of my understanding and experience of a variety of theories and their application in clinical practice but, this time, I had a firm theoretical framework in TA into which I could integrate much of my new learning. I am now registered with the UK Council for Psychotherapy as an integrative psychotherapist.

Throughout this time, I have been in individual and group psychotherapy and have experienced being on the receiving end of psychodynamic psychotherapy, transactional analysis, gestalt, primal integration and existential psychotherapy. I see my own therapy and supervision as essential to my continuing development and understanding as a psychotherapist.

There are many common elements within these different theoretical approaches but, from my experience both as client and psychotherapist, the most crucial common denominator is the relationship between psychotherapist and client. For me, the relationship *is* the psychotherapy. The theory is helpful only in service of the relationship created for the benefit of the client. Here again, I find TA a useful integrative model for describing and keeping track of the relationship in its working-alliance, person-to-person, reparative or transferential aspects.

With this emphasis upon the therapeutic relationship, my major misgiving in writing about working with Charlie is that there is no actual relationship in which to work. Inevitably, much will be missing, but what I hope to present, even without an actual relationship, is my personal approach to psychotherapy using TA as an integrative framework. I would also like to emphasize that this is inevitably a speculative outline of what I would or might do in working with Charlie. In reality, much of the process of the psychotherapy will rely not only upon the developing relationship but also upon what Charlie brings to each session, what she wants to focus on moment by moment. With this in mind, I hope the reader will forgive any impression of a predetermined, linear direction or expectation which may be given through the absence of the real, evolving and unfolding process of face-to-face psychotherapy.

In common with many theories of personality, TA works on the premise that, in response to our childhood experiences, we develop patterns of thinking, feeling and acting which can affect the rest of our lives. Much of these early beginnings then become lost to awareness. TA has a particular way of describing this process of personality and relational development using its own vocabulary. Its methodology is based upon the facilitation of awareness in order to achieve greater spontaneity and intimacy. I have listed a range of books at the end of this chapter for those readers interested in learning more about this approach.

Further information requested

How would you describe your general health?
I wanted to ascertain how Charlie's health may interfere with or enhance ongoing psychotherapy, how her current emotional/psychological state is based in, or influenced by, her physical health and whether any physical problems might preclude certain expressive/active approaches. I specifically wanted to ascertain if her childhood pattern of illness had recurred in her adult life. Her response, 'Now? I'm very healthy', indicated a contrast to her poor health as a child. This, along with previous information, indicated that her present state of physical health would neither interfere with her psychotherapy nor need special focus.

Are you currently on any medication? If so, what?
Was Charlie's psychological/biological state one which may affect the psychotherapy? Charlie was on no medication.

Have you previously had any counselling or psychotherapy? If so, for how long? What kind of therapy was this? Was the treatment beneficial? In what way?
These questions were intended to explore how Charlie had used and might now use psychotherapy beneficially, what approaches may be more helpful and whether hers is a chronic problem (is she representing the same problem?). In the event, Charlie had not had any previous experience of counselling or psychotherapy.

Why have you come to therapy at this particular time?
Charlie's response indicated that there were no acute current events that had precipitated her coming to psychotherapy but rather a realization that she had been ignoring herself and her needs for some time. Seeing her thirteen-year-old daughter so happy, confident and outgoing and having a good mother–daughter relationship, Charlie had begun to compare her own childhood, especially her early teenage years, with that of her daughter: 'I think seeing her growing up and seeing how differently from me she's turned out made me aware that I wasn't really coping as well as I thought I was. I thought, "I've put it all behind me and I can cope with it", and then something brings it all back and I get angry. I get upset. It's just buried really. I've not come to terms with any of it'.

What do you want to achieve?
Having explored the reasons for coming to psychotherapy, this question focuses on the desired outcome. It is the beginning of

making a contract for change. I need to ask myself, can I help Charlie achieve what she wants? Do I have the particular skills or experience to facilitate such change or should I refer her on to someone who does? Is Charlie's goal a realistic one or do we need to see if we can reach agreement upon a more realistic outcome?

Charlie's wants were realistic and fell within my own area of competence. Generally, she was wanting to be more self-confident. In particular, she wanted to deal better with authority figures, to feel better about herself and accept others' positive response to her.

She identified an undermining and critical internal voice. She said, 'I'd like it to be my voice . . . I still experience it as my mother's voice' (identifying an Introjected Parent ego state). This introject tells her that whatever she does, she is 'an inadequate mother and a thoroughly useless person'. Charlie wants to do things because she wants to do them, 'not because she's telling me to do it'.

What are your expectations of psychotherapy? What are your expectations of me?
Charlie said she would like to find out more about herself even though she might find this difficult. Her expectations are realistic. She is prepared for the challenge of psychotherapy. She added, 'If I could find out where I'm responsible for how I am, I could perhaps take responsibility for myself' – a wonderful description of the aim of humanistic psychotherapy with its emphasis upon responsibility.

Do you foresee any particular difficulties with me or the therapy?
In this context, a difficult one for Charlie to answer as we have not met, but she may have had impressions of my style or approach from the questions I have asked. As it is, Charlie replied that she foresaw no difficulties.

How will you and I know when you have achieved your therapeutic goal? What will we notice about you that will be different?
These questions attempt to provide some tangible measure to the outcome of the psychotherapy as well as to further clarify the goal. Charlie replied that she did not know. I will need to explain the reason for the question and explore the possible ways in which we could both make an assessment of the outcome.

You seem to have doubts about becoming autonomous – what do you see as your attitude to change?
Charlie had said, 'I would like to be autonomous . . . but I don't think I ever will be now', reflecting her lack of confidence in herself

– the very aspect she is wanting to work on in psychotherapy. Her reply contained similar hesitation: 'I would like to think it was possible. In fact, I do think it is possible. No, theoretically I think it's possible but in relation to myself I think perhaps it isn't. I suppose I would like to change but I don't know how to. And yes, I do think sometimes that it isn't possible for me to change. Then again, I wouldn't be here if I really thought that, would I?'

I get the impression that your mother had mixed feelings about you – would you say some more about this?
While concerned that her mother's side of the story may be different, Charlie described her own experience: 'I don't see that she ever did or said, or even ever implied, anything that was other than quite negative'. It seems to me that Charlie has a strength of character (perhaps, manifested in her rebellion) to have survived such an experience of all-pervasive negativity towards her.

You say, 'I must have done something' – do you have any immediate (however vague) thoughts or fantasies about what this might have been?
Like all children with negative experiences of their parents, Charlie seeks some explanation of her mother's behaviour towards her and looks to herself for the answer. These 'explanations' become part of the person's 'life script', the beliefs they hold about themselves which influence their life through into adulthood. Charlie responded, 'I used to think it was more what I was than what I had done': first, that she was a girl not a boy; second, that she was not the kind of girl mother could dress up like a pretty doll; and third, that she had different interests from her mother. She also has a vague feeling that she might have *done* something too: 'Perhaps I did something, something unforgivable, and I just don't remember that at all'. However, she seems to think that her illness and her father's death through illness are related. I am reminded of what she said in her interview with Michael: 'It's almost as if as I got stronger he got weaker. Almost as if I had in some way caused it'. Such a powerful and frightening belief clearly needs addressing in the psychotherapy.

TA life script questionnaire

1 *What five aspects of your personality do you most like?*
'Intelligence, humour, sensitivity, unselfishness, open-mindedness'. These are the positive aspects upon which we will be able to draw in our work together.

2 *What five aspects of your personality do you most dislike?*
'Indecisiveness, unassertiveness, laziness, insecurity, easily discouraged'. These negative aspects further identify areas connected with Charlie's lack of confidence. Some of these may be her script beliefs (part of her racket system), which reinforce her script and maintain her frame of reference as an unconfident person. 'Laziness' is a pejorative term, most likely introjected from her mother.

3 *What did you have to do to try to please your mother?*
'If I knew the answer to this I might be happier now'. Charlie reaffirms that nothing satisfied her mother.

4 *What did you do that seemed to displease her most?*
'Being lazy'. Charlie confirms the introjection hypothesized above.

5 *What did you have to do to try to please your father/stepfather?*
[*no response*]

6 *What did you do that seemed to displease him most?*
'He died too long ago – no memory'.

7 *What is the 'bad' feeling you have most frequently?*
'Guilt'. TA defines a 'racket' feeling as a feeling substituted for the original feelings that were not allowed expression in childhood and by which we now maintain our script. I hypothesize that Charlie reinforces her lack of confidence by feeling guilty. She may undermine or discount her anger, fear or sadness in the present by substituting guilt.

8 *Have you ever had the experience of feeling 'trapped' or 'stuck' in a situation? If so, briefly describe such a situation.*
'No'. This question is designed to further explore the rackets or games (those familiar 'here I go again' situations) which Charlie may, outside of her awareness, keep rerunning and thereby reinforce her script. I think my phrasing of the question did not make this clear enough and I am likely to return to it in further work with Charlie.

9 *What has been the happiest/most enjoyable/most exciting occasion in your life?*
'The birth of my three children'. Charlie chooses these positive experiences of birth which, poignantly, are in marked contrast to her own birth and her mother's response to her.

10 *What have you been told concerning your birth?*
In her interview with Michael, Charlie has already told of how she was unwanted (at all and as a girl), unloved and unaccepted, all of which must have had a profound effect upon her view of herself and the development of her life script. In answer to this more specific question, she tells the 'story' she has been told – 'it's a family joke' – about how her mother, thinking she had wind, sat for hours on the outside lavatory until Charlie's grandmother got up and, realizing what this 'coming and going' pain really was, panicking, dragged her daughter into the house and sent grandfather to 'phone for an ambulance. Grandmother put sheets on the living room floor but replaced them with others once she recognized they were 'her very best sheets'. Charlie was born before the ambulance arrived: 'Everybody teases me that I was in such a hurry to get there'.

I will discuss with Charlie what this 'joke' means to her, with its implications of her mother's ignorance/unpreparedness/unacceptance of her imminent birth, the confusion of the signs of her arrival with 'wind', the associations of mother going to the lavatory (a place of emptying and elimination), the speed and panic and, not least, even amidst the panic, grandmother deliberating on the use of her very best sheets. I wonder how this family story of her arrival in the world affected Charlie's self-esteem. There is certainly no indication of joy, delight or welcome. Indeed, she hardly figures in the story.

11 *What would others write on your tombstone?*
'She left nothing behind'. Part of maintaining our script involves holding beliefs about how others see us. This question often elicits such beliefs. Charlie's reply needs clarification. It could be interpreted in several ways: materialistically, existentially, symbolically, spiritually, and so on. On the one hand, it could mean she sees her life as worthless, but on the other, it could mean she sees herself as reaching a point of completion with no loose ends to be tidied up (which might be significantly connected to mother's obsession with tidiness). However, such speculations need to be discussed with Charlie.

12 *What would you like to include in your own epitaph?*
'She will be remembered'. This question can clarify how one sees oneself and what aspirations one may have. I remember Charlie's daughter, who was described as 'famous throughout the school' when Charlie was comparing herself with her daughter. Perhaps Charlie is saying she wants to be noticed, accepted and be significant to others in the way she was not as a child. Again, I will need to discuss this with Charlie.

13 *If you could have three wishes, what would they be?*
'My children to have long and happy lives. That I and my mother could understand each other. A Labour government'. This is an exploration of aspirations and of lacks and losses. Charlie's wishes seem to have a common theme. The first is the wish *of* a caring mother, the second may be the wish *for* a caring mother, while the last may be the wish for a society that reflects such caring.

14 *What was your favourite fairy story/legend (if it was Little Red Riding Hood, was it your grandfather's version)?*
'Robin Hood'. As children we often identify with roles and storylines which reflect our own script decisions. I will need to discuss Charlie's version and understanding of the Robin Hood story to see which elements have meaning for her. I speculate that the story has personal and political significance in its theme of reclaiming from the rich and caring for the poor.

15 *Whose life do you wish you could emulate (real or fictional)?*
'I'd like to write like the Brontës but live like Maid Marion'. I will explore what it is about the Brontë's writing (and which novels) Charlie admires, which may be qualities she is aspiring towards in her life. I am aware that the imaginative and creative Brontë sisters first wrote under male pseudonyms. I am curious to know what qualities Marion represents for Charlie. I speculate on bravery, courage, rebellion, excitement and, again, caring.

Assessment

When reading what Charlie had to say at her interview and her subsequent replies to my questions, I was aware of feeling in tune with her. There were many similarities between her experience as a child and my own and, while aware of the pitfalls of over-identifying (and of the differences in our experience), I felt an empathy with her which I judged would enhance our work together. In addition to this positive Child to Child counter-transference response, I was also aware on several occasions as I read, particularly of her critical and rejecting mother, of my own 'Goodenough Parent' mode and feeling nurturing and supportive towards her. I did not judge this to be a 'Rescuer' role in response to a 'Victim' but an adult response to a hurting child.

   My initial and therefore tentative analysis of Charlie's ego states helps to provide an overall picture of what we might find useful and important points of focus later in our work:

Charlie's Introjected Parent ego states

Maternal introject

- *Rejecting*: told Charlie she would have had an abortion, attempted abortion with gin and hot bath, never saying she was wanted, should have been a boy, boy's name, sent away at five years old: 'She didn't love me'.
- *Uncaring*: unfavourable comparisons with sister, accusations of hypochondria, library book incidents, unwillingness to listen to Charlie – doesn't notice or care.
- *Critical and controlling*: Charlie's emerging sexuality as a teenager, negative attitude to being a woman – 'unpleasant', 'the curse', 'women suffer', 'men only want one thing', 'tarty', should have hair cut and dress how mother wanted. 'This voice in my head all the time is telling me, "It doesn't matter what I do, I will never be a worthwhile person" . . . it's my mother's voice . . . it's her facial expression, and I still feel controlled by that', obsessive tidiness.
- *Passive acceptance*: 'Life isn't fair, you have to put up with it', (mother's violent second marriage), 'What you must do now is just forget it' (Charlie's abortion).

Paternal introject

Charlie's father seems a shadowy, unavailable figure even before he died. He was away on National Service when she was born. When she was two and a half he became ill. He died when she was five, which she does not remember, but may be seen as another 'rejection' in her life.

Other possible introjects

- *Foster parents when Charlie was five years old*: kind and caring. Charlie's visit to the Monument with the husband seems an exciting and positive experience which, treasured in her child ego state, may also indicate some introjection of goodenough parenting.
- *Grandfather*: another possible positive introject. He seems to have been very fond of Charlie, an inventive storyteller (albeit for propaganda purposes!) and was clearly influential in Charlie's socialist development. He was supportive and protective of her against her mother's criticisms. Both foster-father and grandfather provide Charlie with positive, nurturing counterbalances to mother's inadequacies.
- *First stepfather*: Charlie was eighteen when her mother remarried.

Her maturity and the negative response she had to this 'absolute bastard' ('unpleasant, objectionable and opinionated') deems the possibility of introjection remote.

Charlie's Archaic Child ego states

To diagnose specific ego states (coherent sets of feelings, thoughts and behaviours), their developmental age and chronology, in further work with Charlie, I will need to use the four methods of TA diagnosis, namely behavioural, social, historical and phenomenological. Her experiences in early childhood of rejection, criticism, separation, loss and illness, as well as her positive experiences of her grandfather and foster-parents, will need particular focus. What follows here is a general view of the contents of Charlie's Child ego state, which, for convenience and brevity, I describe under three separate but inevitably interrelated headings:

- *Child feelings*: hurt, sadness, frustration and anger in response to her mother's criticism/insensitivity/lack of love and unfavourable comparisons with her sister. Guilt following anger or rebellion. Grief at loss of father, foster-parents and grandfather, grief at rejection. (Note that Charlie's husband is experienced in bereavement counselling.) Nervousness (as observed in interview with Michael), lack of confidence, insecurity. Feels she should apologize for herself. Anger over treatment at school.
- *Child thoughts*: I am not wanted/worthwhile/important/of value, I am a nuisance/difficult/argumentative, etc. (all attributions given by mother but reflected in the present, e.g. by 'wasting your time' remark in initial interview). I am unwanted/unloved/uncared for ('I was a mistake'), I should have been a boy. It's my fault. There is something wrong with me. I caused my father's and my grandparents' deaths ('As I got stronger he got weaker'; 'All of mine [grandparents] seemed to die at the same time as I got noticeably stronger'). If I'm weak/ill, maybe mother will love me ('weak and helpless, that was just how she wanted me to be'). Conversely, I should be strong (like my sister). Others think I'm stupid (experience of teacher at primary school), which she still projects on to others (her friend Barbara, for example). People will leave me (childhood belief reflected in present relationship with husband). I must try hard to please my mother (but it's impossible so I'll rebel).
- *Child behaviours*: rebels against mother and her 'shoulds': 'What does my mother want me to do? Right, I'll do the opposite!' At other times, feeling guilty, she tries to please her by doing what

she wants: 'I'm doing it because my internal mother tells me to and makes me feel guilty'. Behaves towards others in a way that leads them to think she dislikes them (with Barbara, for example).

Charlie's Integrated Adult ego states

Charlie's ability to respond appropriately to the needs of here-and-now reality are shown both in the self-aware manner in which she conducts herself during the interview and in much of the life she describes. She clearly possesses many fine qualities, which she has employed to develop and maintain a relationship, to bring up three children who seem to be successful and happy, and to achieve and enjoy a responsible job. She says, 'It's only when I'm at work that I feel like an adult person', but outside the office she regresses 'back to the little girl my mother made'. I suspect this is in part a Parent contamination of her Adult, reflecting her mother's discounting, for she seems articulate, intelligent, caring, thoughtful, humorous and lively, shows a fluidity in her feelings and is able to form friendships (despite her lack of confidence) and gain the respect of others outside of her work too. Her desire is to achieve being in an Integrated Adult ego state, autonomously choosing what she wants to do.

Main intrapsychic dynamic

From the interview with Michael, Charlie has already indicated her difficulty in disengaging herself from the internal influence of her mother's criticisms. Though she does not always comply with her mother's wishes, she still adapts to them rebelliously in her Archaic Child ego state. Charlie's Introjected Parent invokes her Child to 'try hard' (with the concomitant injunctions 'don't succeed', 'don't think' and 'don't') and 'please me' (with the concomitant injunctions 'don't be you', 'don't be a child', 'don't be important'). The injunction 'don't exist' pervades all. In response, Charlie may at times try to please her internal Parent but, in the face of the impossibility of this, feeling inadequate, incompetent and hopeless, frustratedly rebel. This, in turn, displeases her Parent and her Child feels guilty.

Interpersonal dynamics

In relation to others (shown most clearly in her relationship with her friend Barbara, but also with her husband), Charlie projects her critical and rejecting Parent on to them and responds from her Child ego state with the beliefs about herself listed above under

'Child thoughts' and the associated feelings and behaviours. In this way, she maintains and reinforces her script. With Barbara, despite the evidence to the contrary, she puts herself in an 'I'm not OK/You are OK' position ('I could not believe she could possibly like me'), acts in a way that Barbara perceives as Charlie not liking her and risks inviting the thing she fears – criticism and rejection by the other. Similarly, she projects a rejecting Parent on to her husband and in so doing risks inviting his irritation with her – 'The mildest row . . . and I think he's going to leave me, and he finds that very irritating'.

Personality adaptation

My initial, tentative diagnosis, based upon Paul Ware's (1983) work on personality adaptations, is that Charlie's adaptation is one of an 'enthusiastic overreactor', traditionally called 'hysteric' (Joines 1986). I base this on the feelings she expresses during her interview, her dramatic and expressive style of communication, and her tendency to be over-inclusive in what she is talking about to the point of forgetting where she started (which Michael describes at the start of the initial interview as 'a form of expression that had begun to lose substance'). She also seems to be able to talk about traumatic experiences with little difficulty or affect. This hypothesis indicates that the 'open door' to working with Charlie is through her feelings. This is where Charlie and I will make contact and establish rapport. The integration of her Adult thinking is the 'target door' to be reached via her feelings. The 'trap door' is her behaviour (Charlie is doing all she can already to 'please me/others' [mother], is therefore vulnerable in this area and is initially likely to rebel against behavioural interventions), eventually to be reached through the integration of her feeling and thinking.

Therapeutic possibilities

The main indications of successful therapy with Charlie are that she has realistic goals and expectations and is willing to take responsibility for herself. There is no suggestion that she is expecting some 'magic' solution, nor that the therapist holds the secret to her changing. I get the impression that she is prepared for a cooperative collaboration between herself and the therapist. She is also open to talking about herself and shows a psychological sophistication in her self-awareness. I especially see her clear identification of her maternal introject ('my mother's voice') as assisting analysis and work with her intrapsychic and interpersonal dynamics. Further, her list of positive aspects – 'intelligence, humour, sensitivity, unselfishness, open-mindedness' – are good indications for our work together. In particular, I see a sense of humour (as distinct from self-mockery or 'gallows' laughter) both in the client and the therapist as a vital, growth-enhancing component of psychotherapy. There are also several examples of Charlie's capacity for relationship (despite her lack of confidence) with family and friends, which indicate that she is likely to engage usefully in the therapeutic relationship.

As I have said previously, I think Charlie has a certain strength of character to have achieved what she has in her life and to be functioning so well despite her mother's negativity and continuing influence upon her self-confidence. I do not think her being in her early forties mitigates against a successful outcome, as I believe this age is a necessary time for reconsideration of one's life course: reviewing the past and looking towards the future from the vantage-point of mid-life. Particularly now that Charlie's children are teenagers and, therefore, experimenting with independence and self-direction, I think it is an important time for Charlie to experiment with her own as she nears the end of 'at home' parenting, which often leaves parents in the void of an 'open-ended' script.

I think TA theory – structural, transactional, game and racket analysis – could facilitate a clarity of understanding of how Charlie transacts both in internal dialogue and in the world, highlight the repeated patterns by which she reinforces her early script decisions about her lack of self-worth (and her concomitant lack of confidence) and, through the processes of decontamination, deconfusion, self-reparenting and redecision, bring about the desired change. What I can usefully bring to enhance the success of the therapy is my general knowledge and experience of working with people whose self-esteem is diminished through constant criticism throughout childhood and, more specifically, my knowledge, skills and experience of working within a TA framework with clients who have this and related problems. Like Charlie, I have a sense of humour. I anticipate appropriate laughter and enjoyment facilitating our work together – not as an avoidance of more serious and difficult times, but as an important and necessary human expression within relationships, including therapeutic ones.

I am optimistic of a successful outcome to psychotherapy with Charlie. This is not to suggest that it would be without difficulties or distress as it would be for any client attempting to change the patterns and adaptations they have evolved in childhood. I will refer to these potential difficulties later.

The course of therapy

Establishing the therapeutic relationship

The relationship *is* the psychotherapy. The course of therapy will depend upon Charlie feeling safe enough within that relationship to talk about, explore and experience herself fully and openly. Developing a working alliance will be the first step towards creating such a relationship, with an emphasis upon clarifying the goals, providing a clear and consistent time structure, fee structure, holiday arrangements, and so on. Such considerations will assist Charlie and I in developing a trusting Adult-to-Adult relationship to which we can return even from the most negative transference. She will need to feel listened to and accepted. In this respect, the relationship will provide a reparative experience of being seen, heard and accepted, a relationship contrary to much of her childhood experience. Conversely, through the transferential relationship, it is likely that at times Charlie will see me as yet another abandoning and rejecting figure with whom she cannot get it right and with whom she feels unconfident. Through the working alliance, the person-to-person relationship, my sharing (when appropriate) of my counter-transference reactions, and structural and transactional analysis, we will work towards dissolving the transference in the course of our work together. A similar working-through will be necessary if Charlie moves into an idealized transference, seeing me as the desired all-giving perfect parent. Charlie's often rebellious and counter-dependent adaptation to her mother may cover a deep yearning for this sort of caring.

While mindful of the undulating, shifting, interweaving, sometimes cyclical (sometimes stuck!) nature of the process of psychotherapy, I will draw upon transactional analysis to provide a general map of the treatment direction within which to work with Charlie and to assess movement towards our goal. I emphasize that this is necessarily a very brief and general overview of what *might* happen in the psychotherapy.

Contracting

Charlie and I will need to clarify what she wants to achieve. In general, she has indicated she wants to be more self-confident. In particular, she wants to deal better with authority figures, to feel better about herself and accept others' positive response to her. We will discuss how we can make these goals more specific. If she were to be dealing better with authority figures and feeling better about herself, what would she be doing differently?

There are also several indications in the transcript that Charlie is wanting to make wider changes in herself and in her life which would constitute an 'autonomy contract', the focus of which would be changing her intrapsychic structure.

Dealing with confusion

Decontamination

The interference into the here-and-now Adult ego state by either introjected or archaic material is known as 'contamination'. The process of decontamination will involve the identifying and separating out of Charlie's historic ego states from her Adult ego state. I have tentatively suggested the possible contents of Charlie's ego states earlier. These will need to be assessed and verified by Charlie in the course of structural analysis. We might experiment with using three chair exercises for her to experience the feelings, thoughts and behaviours of each of her three types of ego states and help separate them out. For example, we might address her lack of confidence as a double (Child/Parent) contamination of her Adult, identifying her critical parental introjections in operation and her concomitant re-experiencing of helplessness in her Child – both influencing her current experience in certain situations (especially with authority figures). Clearly, this is an ongoing process, my task being to bring Charlie's attention to statements she may make within the sessions (or describe from outside situations) in which she may assume an Adult ego state where historic ego states are in operation.

Deconfusion

With the strengthening of Charlie's Adult brought about by decontamination and the utilization of her self-nurturing and support, we will give particular attention to Charlie's Child ego states and find ways of allowing her to express those thoughts, feelings and behaviours which were not allowed expression during childhood. It is likely that Charlie will need to release her feelings of hurt, grief, sadness, fear and anger (especially in response to mother's rejection and criticism), and express her thoughts and actions which she may have repressed at the time. This may take the form of enactment, using an empty chair to symbolically represent her mother (or others) in order to facilitate catharsis, not just through her words but also through her bodily movement and emotional expression. The aim of this process is to release the energy in Charlie's natural Child and allow her safe expression, as well as to reach an understanding of the decisions that Charlie made as a child and discover how and why she may be maintaining them. Such work is likely to clarify her internal conflicts especially in relation to her mother (as already suggested in the section on intrapsychic dynamics) and assist in further structural, racket and script analysis.

Conflict resolution

Allowing Charlie's natural Child expression will bring her up against her internalized mother's (and others') prohibitions, criticisms and injunctions and her own decisions and beliefs about herself which have maintained her lack of confidence – the 'impasses' of TA theory. In this respect, we might usefully employ redecision techniques based upon the work of Bob and Mary Goulding (1979). Working through these internal conflicts towards making new decisions will involve the continuing strengthening of Charlie's Adult as an ally for her Child, requiring also that my Parent mode be stronger than Charlie's Parent ego state in order to provide the necessary permission, protection and potency within the therapeutic relationship. I believe these elements to be the main vehicles for change rather than any techniques. Where techniques are employed, I see them as secondary to the relationship, assisting change subtly and gradually.

Attending to the deficit

On the way to, in support of and beyond the redecisions that Charlie might make, we will identify areas where there is a lack of developmentally needed experience. Evidently, there are gross deficiencies in Charlie's very early experiences of being wanted, loved and accepted as herself and as a girl by her mother. We can also see later deficiencies in being listened to and given importance, of being recognized and positively accepted as a sexual being, of having wants and needs independent of her mother. Again, I see the therapeutic relationship itself as being potentially reparative. Additionally, we might identify very specific deficits and contract for 'spot-reparenting' of deficiencies to be addressed by me. For example, at the age of two and a half, when Charlie recovered from whooping cough, her father became ill and she felt responsible for this and his later death. It may be that Charlie's Child of this time is lacking the necessary reassurance and information from a grown-up that this is not the case. We might, therefore, having explored her original experience and confusion, contract to do a psychodramatic enactment in which I, as her advocate, 'visit' her during her convalescence and talk to her about the separateness of her own illness to that of her father.

Such reparative experiences are not an end in themselves but a step towards Charlie developing and expanding her own self-nurturing qualities in support of her Child and her grown-up self. She has many positive qualities which she uses towards her children and others. Our task would be to identify these qualities, add to her repertoire and find ways that Charlie can use them to nurture and support herself – in particular, in those areas in which she is lacking confidence and self-esteem.

Relearning

Charlie needs to put into practice the changes she has made. This is likely to involve using her self-nurturing to support her new decisions in her dealings with others whom she sees as in authority, in particular in her current relationship with her mother. Later in our work, we might incorporate homework assignments with specific tasks to be undertaken in those areas in which she was previously lacking confidence. In this way, she will be both practising her new behaviours as well as assessing them. One area might be that of making new friends from an 'I'm OK/You're OK' position rather than her previous one-down approach as with her friend Barbara. We will need to check out how confident she is feeling, what archaic thinking might still be interfering, what she is still projecting onto others, what ulterior messages she may still be sending to invite rejection and what further work may be needed to address these issues. If feeling confident and successful, we will also take time to celebrate her achievements and build upon them in other important areas of her life.

Ending

Having assessed the achievement of our contracts, Charlie and I will agree upon a suitable date for ending the therapy. In the light of other endings in Charlie's life (her father's death, her separation from her mother and then her foster parents, and the death of her grandparents) and especially in view of her past belief that her growing strength in some way leads to the weakening and eventual loss of others, it will be important that we end sensitively with time to express thoughts and feelings, to take stock and to celebrate our work together.

Problem areas

Charlie seems uncertain as to whether she can change: 'I would like to be autonomous ... but I don't think I ever will be now'. She seems to suggest that it is possible for others to change and that 'in theory' change is achievable but not for her. This ambivalence is in marked contrast to her more positive view of the changes she wants to make, her realistic expectations of therapy and her preparedness for taking responsibility. This may reflect what is known in TA as a Type 3 impasse, where in an early Child ego state she is believing, 'I've always been like this, this is really me, I can't be otherwise'. Clearly, if unaddressed, this could undermine any attempts at change within the psychotherapy. We will need to energize her natural tendency towards growth and change in order to challenge and refute this early decision as well as later reinforcing beliefs and introjections. I do not see this as an insurmountable problem, but I think it will take some time to help Charlie shift such a fundamental attitude towards herself and, in the light of her assertion that she is 'easily discouraged', will require the early development of a 'holding environment' through a strong and stable working alliance in which Charlie can allow herself to feel discouraged (and explore her experience) yet remain committed to the therapeutic process. If this is not achieved, I think Charlie might leave therapy prematurely and construe it as another reinforcing experience of the 'don't succeed' aspect of her script.

In the area of the transference relationship, there is the potential problem of Charlie seeing me as a critical Parent who (like mother) is impossible to please however hard she tries. Here again, Charlie may re-experience her sense of inadequacy and lack of self-worth and defend against this by moving into a rebellious position which may involve quitting the therapy. However, it is not the transference itself which is the problem (in fact, the transference provides a useful vehicle for working through her archaic experiences). My concern is more with Charlie possibly acting out the transference by ending the therapy. Again, the strength of our non-transferential relationship, particularly the Adult-to-Adult aspect of our working alliance, will be crucial. Charlie will need to feel safe enough within that relationship to move into Child–Parent transactions with me – for example, to be angry and rebellious, to feel rejected and criticized – without losing the connection of our established working partnership.

As with Charlie's transference, my counter-transference reactions are essential and constructive aspects of the therapy as well as potential problem areas. How I am feeling, thinking and behaving in response to Charlie will be useful indicators of her intrapsychic and interpersonal dynamics. However, I will need to carefully monitor my reactions and make sure that they are not my own unresolved Parent or Child ego states and that they are in the service of Charlie's therapy, not my own. I have mentioned earlier that there are several aspects of Charlie's childhood experience which are similar to mine and that this may be useful in my empathic responses to her. On the other hand, I will need to be vigilant in not over-identifying, making assumptions based on my experience rather than hers, or confusing my Child feelings with hers. Further, inasmuch as Charlie's Parent Introject is punitive towards her Child, that same potential is available towards others when Charlie is in her Parent ego state. Though I get little impression of this from the transcript, I will need to keep my Child protected while also keeping my responses available for understanding and empathizing with Charlie's Child experiences. Similarly, I will need to monitor my own Parent responses in order to avoid unwittingly either enacting my own punitive Parent or allowing myself to act as Charlie's mother.

In my earlier assessment, I was aware of my own 'Goodenough Parent' mode and of feeling nurturing and supportive towards her. I stated that I did not judge this to be a 'Rescuer' role in response to a 'Victim', but an adult response to a hurting child. I was already anticipating the potential need to avoid playing a Rescuer role whereby I might keep Charlie in a dependent and powerless Victim position. This is a fine balance to keep and one which may, at times, prove difficult. It will be important to make sure as far as is possible that any reparative work (including that which occurs intrinsically within the therapeutic relationship) is addressed from an 'I'm OK/You're OK' position, avoiding undermining the strengths and qualities which Charlie already possesses while at the same time affording her the experience of being cared for and accepted as a person worthy of respect and esteem.

Criteria for successful outcome

The outcome of psychotherapy with Charlie needs to be viewed primarily in the light of the contracts we will make. These are likely to include social change contracts in terms of her self-confidence and dealings with people she sees as authority figures, including her mother, and acceptance of others' positive response to her. She also indicates that she may be wanting to make an Autonomy Contract (see 'Contracting' above), which I see as involving an ongoing, longer-term commitment to the therapeutic process over two or three years on a weekly individual basis, including a period during this time of group psychotherapy, where her transactional patterns can be addressed within the wider context provided by a group.

Taking into account my initial assessment of Charlie and her presenting problems, my consideration of the therapeutic possibilities, and balancing these with the potential problem areas (all of which can only be clarified and verified in the developing therapeutic relationship), I anticipate a mutually challenging, exciting and creative therapeutic process with some tough, intense and perhaps despairing periods in which Charlie may experience both pain and joy in the letting go of her script, reclaiming her Child and achieving autonomy.

I have already referred to the 'reasons' for my prediction of a positive outcome to our work together in earlier sections and will, therefore, not repeat them here. Along with these, I also take account of my more intuitive sense of a constructive outcome. This may seem odd in view of all I have said about the need for an actual relationship. However, in the process of reading, thinking, feeling and writing about how I might approach working with Charlie, I have felt an involvement and engagement (even within this necessarily hypothetical process) which I see as a useful indicator to predicting a successful achievement of her goals.

So how do I conceive of Charlie if the outcome of psychotherapy is successful? What might it mean for her to be autonomous? I see first and foremost, a confident, decisive woman being pro-active in her life and responding to situations from an integrated Adult ego state rather than her Child or Parent. In particular, the 'voice in her head' will be her own. Though there may be times when she hears her mother's voice, she will none the less be able to deal with this, protect her Child, avoid adaptation through compliance or rebellion, and assess the situation for herself. Her house will be tidy or untidy according to what she wants! She will relate to others from an 'I'm OK/You're OK' position, seeing herself and others as human beings worthy of respect and consideration and be both stroke-receiving as well as stroke-giving. This will include relating to her mother with self-respect and confidence without feeling compelled to please her. Her mother may not change in her understanding of Charlie, but Charlie will be able to relate to her without feeling inadequate, 'lazy', guilty or at fault, seeing her in the light of her own script and her experiences as a child and as a very young mother with her inevitable inadequacies. She will not see herself as responsible through her illness for her father's death.

I do not know if 'she will be remembered' or be famous like her daughter. She will, however, inevitably make good contact with others and experience her own significance more fully. With her qualities of 'intelligence, humour, sensitivity, unselfishness and open-mindedness', she may indeed write like the Brontë sisters. As for Maid Marion, perhaps she is already there. And a Labour government?

Well, unfortunately (or perhaps, fortunately), some things are outside the bounds of psychotherapy.

Summary

I have aimed to illustrate my own personal approach to psychotherapy with Charlie based in the theoretical concepts of TA, which I believe is a useful framework within which to integrate humanistic, behavioural and psychodynamic approaches to helping people change. Despite the lack of an actual relationship with Charlie, I hope I have emphasized the centrality of relationship to the psychotherapeutic process. I have attempted to show the mutuality of the therapeutic endeavour in terms of the skills, qualities, responsibilities and experiences we both bring to the process of psychotherapy in order to help Charlie make the changes she desires. The main difficulty in this task of writing ahead of the therapy has been to avoid the notion of a restricted, linear and predetermined aspect to the process. In actuality, there is much that is idiosyncratic, lateral, illogical, surprising and unpredictable about the process of psychotherapy and, therefore, could only be described in retrospect once Charlie had completed her therapy.

I would like to wish Charlie well in her psychotherapy and her future life and thank her for providing this exciting and valuable opportunity to explore my own approach to psychotherapy. My thanks also to Maria Gilbert and Charlotte Sills for their supportive and helpful 'supervision' of this chapter.

Further reading

Berne, E. (1961). *Transactional Analysis in Psychotherapy*. New York: Grove Press.

Berne, E. (1972). *What Do You Say After You Say Hello?* New York: Grove Press.

Clarkson, P. (1992). *Transactional Analysis Psychotherapy: An Integrated Approach*. London: Tavistock/Routledge.

Goulding, R. and Goulding, M. (1979). *Changing Lives through Redecision Therapy*. New York: Brunner/Mazel.

Joines, V. (1986). Using redecision therapy with different personality adaptations. *Transactional Analysis Journal*, Vol. 16, No. 3.

Kahn, M. (1991). *Between Therapist and Client: The New Relationship*. New York: Freeman.

Lapworth, P., Sills, C. and Fish, S. (1993). *Transactional Analysis Counselling*. Oxford: Winslow Press.

Stewart, I. (1989). *Transactional Analysis Counselling in Action*. London: Sage.
Ware, P. (1983). Personality adaptations. *Transactional Analysis Journal*, Vol. 3, No. 1.

FRANK MARGISON

PSYCHOANALYTIC PSYCHOTHERAPY

The therapist

There are several elements to my self-description as a therapist, and the discussion of my approach to Charlie will develop these. I can be described as a psychoanalytically or psychodynamically oriented therapist in my main practice. I am a teacher and supervisor on local trainings, which focus on awareness of transference and unconscious communication. That description of me is accurate but only partial.

I work wholly within a National Health Service (NHS) specialist psychotherapy unit in Manchester (where I am also clinical director of the psychiatric service). I try to help each individual to make a choice between a variety of therapies, including behavioural-cognitive therapy, creative therapies and couple therapy, as well as psychoanalytic therapy. Within my main orientation there is also a choice between brief focused methods and longer-term exploration. I am acting to some extent as an advisor or broker to Charlie, trying to help her to choose between different approaches. I am uneasily aware that in a real assessment I would be constrained by the resources available.

The main influence on me comes from my own training and supervision with Robert Hobson, who described and developed his 'conversational model' (Hobson 1985). It is difficult to summarize briefly, but is essentially a depth psychology drawing on Jungian and psychoanalytic concepts, expressed with a focus on the 'here and now' relationship within a shared feeling language. When I started my training with Robert Hobson in 1977, his views were at the edge of contemporary psychodynamic practice, whereas his work is now nearer to mainstream psychodynamic practice. He was also a pioneer in developing short-term therapy and applying modern educational approaches to teaching psychotherapy skills. He applied video and audio training and skills analysis to his own method, and I was greatly influenced by my own analysis of my sessions using research tools.

A second key personal figure in my development as a therapist has been David Docl, a Unitarian Minister and teacher and writer on depth psychology. He has helped me to see psychotherapy in a much broader context, and to realize that psychotherapy research is a small part of a larger whole and is not limited to the empirical model.

I have continued the tradition of being a researcher/practitioner. I worked for several years as a clinical lecturer and some of my research was on the impact of serious mental illness on mothering. This pushed me into learning more about the early mother–infant relationship. I am now critical of some psychoanalytic models of development, which do not seem to take account of the baby's well-developed capacity to relate. This drew me to see the importance of the work of John Bowlby (1979) on early attachments and also the work of Daniel Stern (1985), who has revised our models of how different aspects of the 'self' develop.

There is a tension between rigorous approaches to research methodology and a personal focus to the work undertaken. I feel this tension to be fruitful and I hope that at least a flavour of this will come through in the discussion 'with Charlie'.

Further information requested

I approached this in the way that I would in my normal clinical work. I asked for Charlie to be given a standard departmental questionnaire. The first part asks for some basic information about family, education, work and any previous treatment. There are also some open-ended questions about how the person sees the problem, or changes he or she hopes for, and a space for any additional material. This is supplemented by two standardized questionnaires, which are used quite widely for both research and clinical audit. The first is a 90-item symptom checklist (Symptom Checklist 90 R), which covers in a systematic way a variety of symptoms primarily to do with mental health. There is also an Inventory of Interpersonal Problems (developed by Len Horowitz), which looks at particular relationship themes.

Pattern of symptoms

The Symptom Checklist 90 R shows a clear pattern to the difficulties Charlie reports. There are standardized ways of reporting this questionnaire which are useful in monitoring progress, but I am using it in a less formal way here to look for patterns of symptoms which will help me to focus our attention during the assessment interview.

Depression

Although the overall level of symptoms is not high, it is clear that the symptoms are mainly of depression:

blaming herself	low energy	'blue'
poor appetite	self-blame	difficulty getting to sleep
early waking	restless sleep	guilt
unpleasant thoughts	mind blank	feeling blocked

However, these symptoms are mainly rated as low ('a little bit'), which means the depression is not severe but it is pervasive and also includes some somatic symptoms of backache, faintness and headache.

Relationships

There are also symptoms about relationships:

• feeling others are to blame,
• lonely even when people present,
• most people can't be trusted,
• people will take advantage,
• others unfriendly,
• not understood.

I was surprised by this cluster, as it does not come out so strongly in the interviews but the extent of alienation from others is often difficult to pick up in a person who generally functions well.

   The *Inventory of Interpersonal Problems* is designed to give a more detailed account of relationship issues. Again the average score is not very high, but looking at the items shows that the main difficulties fall in the areas of being assertive, meeting her own needs, fear of harming others, showing feelings, being affectionate and self-confidence.

Information from the structured questionnaire

The open-ended questionnaire supplemented the information we already have. The initial part of the form fills in personal details which are irrelevant or have been left out to maintain confidentiality.

Family and childhood

The question about family atmosphere elicited the point that it felt varied; sometimes safe refuge and sometimes a feeling of being 'on trial'. Charlie confirmed that she had no memory of her father, a difficult relationship with her mother and was not close to her sister. She had a significant separation of a year in London shortly after her father's death and just before she developed a prolonged illness following whooping cough.

She did not feel either abused or threatened during childhood. The account of her education was straightforward and I noted that she was able to make friends and keep them, but did not like the 'snobbishness or rigid rules' at school.

I wondered whether these themes might appear as transference themes: Will Charlie see me as holding to rigid rules about the structure of the therapy, and will she see me as 'snobbish', or aloof if I do not say a great deal about myself?

Jobs

Her occupational history had been disrupted to some extent by family responsibilities, but she now gains satisfaction from 'doing things well at work', and the only problem was thinking herself to be 'lazy'.

Home life

The question about responsibility in the home brought a reply that she is responsible for all the housework without any statement about why this should be. She again commented that she was 'lazy' and did as little as possible. I noted that I might try to re-frame this as possibly being a thwarted drive towards freedom.

Interests, strengths and current relationships

Charlie commented on a wide range of interests, particularly reading. She identifies a number of positive things about herself, including being intelligent, sympathetic, a good communicator and receptive.

She did not think that there were any persistent relationship problems, other than with her mother. She has had four close friendships
with women and one significant relationship before her marriage
which 'ultimately ended unhappily'. In the current relationship, sex
was usually all right but she commented that her interest was reduced when she was depressed.

Asking about Charlie's strengths helps to keep the area of difficulty in perspective and also to identify resources for her to use
during the therapy.

The relationship with her three children seems positive and the
few worries she mentioned did not seem closely linked to the main
theme, although her role as mother almost certainly will be at some
point.

Health and current problems

Generally, her health is good and she has never had any psychological treatment in the past. The main current problem is of 'guilt
regarding the relationship with my mother' (although later when
asked to sum up her difficulties in one phrase, she said: 'lacking the
courage of my convictions').

Aims

In response to a question about changes she would like, she thought
she would like to be able to respond to people without feeling
useless, but 'doesn't know how!' In response to a specific prompt,
she commented that there was no information which she could not
write down and she chose not to use the space at the end for her
own comments.

Questions asked by the therapist on my behalf

The experience of setting up a number of questions for Michael
Jacobs to ask felt rather strange, and there were a couple of points
that I would like to pursue further but in general the information
was very helpful.

Preferences

I asked a number of questions which are focused on my NHS work,
where I often act as an initial contact point helping people to make
choices between various forms of therapy.

1 *Model of therapy?* My first question was about her preferred model and she responded that she knew most about, and was attracted most to, a psychodynamic approach having studied Freud as part of a psychology course; or possibly a person-centred approach. This preference fits in well with my own personal orientation but she also commented that she knew too little about other methods to express any preference.

2 *Gender of therapist?* Charlie felt that 'authoritative women tend to make me feel a bit intimidated'. She is more comfortable 'relating to a man who is in a position of authority'. She also feared that she might be slightly inhibited with a woman but in the end would not mind working with either. This made me want to follow up with some supplementary questions and to try to link it with her experience 'here and now' in the room with me.

3 Group or individual therapy? Charlie felt that it would be easier to stay quiet in a group and 'not really engage'. She thought it might be easier to let more extrovert people take over and would prefer a one-to-one relationship. In response to this I would have liked to explain a little bit about the way groups work, and that facing such fears in a group setting can be a very creative experience, although in the end the choice would be hers. In practice I would be uneasily aware of the much quicker access to a group than for long-term individual work within my NHS setting, which would be a factor in the choice.

Why now?

Charlie linked the start of her problems in her early teens and the age of her eldest daughter. In fact it was not their similarity but rather their difference that made Charlie aware that 'I wasn't really coping as well as I thought I was'. She had thought that she had 'put it all behind me', but then found things brought it back and she got angry or upset. It made her think that she had just buried her feelings and that she had not come to terms with any of it.

Fears about therapy

There were no particular fears about what might happen in therapy, other than that she might find 'more than I bargained for' and that she might find it more difficult than she had expected to take responsibility for herself.

Knowing when therapy had worked

Charlie was silent when asked how she would know if therapy had been effective. I am aware that this is often the case and I get the person to imagine waking up and taking me through a typical day, highlighting any differences as she meets different people. With this prompt she commented that she would not apologize for herself any more, and would no longer agree openly when inwardly she disagreed. She would also feel more confident to be able to do things and be more able to face the day with a confident outlook. She also felt that she would be more able to take control of things, such as job opportunities, and not just be reactive.

A response as detailed as this is very helpful and gives me confidence that we could work on agreed goals and also know when we had achieved them (see later). In this I think I am different from many psychoanalytic psychotherapists, who would be more concerned primarily with the ability to explore rather than agreeing a destination!

Identifying with stage, book or film characters

She apologized for the 'arrogance' of her reply but 'had a lot of sympathy with Hamlet because of his indecisiveness and his inability to get to grips with what are basically very ordinary family problems really'. She commented about her sexual disgust when her mother married her first stepfather and linked this with Hamlet's feelings. This theme did not appear anywhere else and might have been easier to express in this form. The ability to live imaginatively through another character and the psychological depth of her comment suggest that Charlie will be comfortable with exploring links between different parts of her life.

Dreams

She does not remember many dreams but did recall looking after her daughter's cornet and discovering that she had lost it. The trust had been 'quite an honour and a compliment' and so she was relieved when she woke up.

I would follow up with an invitation to explore the dream, which would give some information about her readiness to consider different meanings. I would be happy to offer my own tentative thoughts such as the identification of her daughter's creativity (and the threat of its loss) with her own 'lost childhood'.

I might try a 'deeper' link with the disguised, possibly aggressive aspect of the dream. As well as the anxiety about restricting her daughter's creativity, there might be an identification with her *mother*, who restricted Charlie's own creativity and ability 'to play'. Naturally, these would be tentative hypotheses to be tried out to see if there is any sense of 'fit' for Charlie.

Myths and 'rules'

The rule that 'others always get ill if you get stronger' had no exception other than her mother. This made me think that the conflict was likely to be deeply rooted.

Being in touch with core feelings

I asked her to imagine wearing the pale blue dress with the broad belt and how she responded to her mother's outrage. Even through a transcript the feeling came through here: 'I just felt really embarrassed, humiliated and upset that she could say things like that about me'. She made a link about buying black patent shoes for her daughter, and noting her mother's different response to her granddaughter. She ends, 'Yes I was really hurt'.

This made me think that there are 'core affects' of *embarrassment* and *humiliation* and that I would need to go back to these in any formulation.

Good figures as internal resources

I asked her about her grandfather, as a good figure in her life, and how he might advise her currently. She commented that he *was* a good figure but rarely gave advice even though he was supportive in other ways.

Impact of the interview

Remembering all of the painful memories of the past felt like a catharsis. She felt that she had thought quite hard in a way she had not done before. She had been able to see that things were not her fault, but also commented to Michael about 'all of these people who were asking all these questions and not knowing her'. She contrasted 'us' not knowing her, even her name, and Michael whom she felt knew so much about her.

This reply seemed particularly interesting. The effort of responding to the stylized questions delivered by Michael to Charlie had been going well, but my question about how it felt with him caused a failure of the 'suspension of disbelief' and strong positive transference material came through. She ends with a plea: 'I have tried to be honest'.

Shortly afterwards she was asked how it had felt 'talking with me here today'. She commented that it felt good, but on the way there that day she had the thought, 'he knows so much about me now'. She had wanted to ask whether he liked her, but felt embarrassed. Her replies were less organized at this point, and then she made a comment about having met him (Michael Jacobs) at a public lecture in the north-west. She had introduced her husband to Michael, and she commented, 'This is my husband . . . Oh my God!', and later thought, 'These are two of the people who probably know me better than anybody else'. This is clearly very conflictual material with an embarrassing and potentially humiliating triangle, which I would have liked to have brought into the psychodynamic formulation.

One concern about contributing this chapter had been a fear that transference material would not develop towards the therapist in a way which could be understood. This material suggests that the evidence is there and can easily be related to the psychodynamic themes.

Priorities

Earlier Charlie had been asked whether her priority was to develop better ways of handling her upset feelings or whether she would want to take the risk of exploring painful feelings further, even though there is no guarantee of success. She replied in an indirect way. She related an anecdote about a friend with a puerperal psychosis. Later her husband was led to say, 'Ah, so insight does help!'

She commented that she is ambivalent about the psychodynamic approach but thought, 'Yes he is right, it does'. She wanted to take the risk of exploring things that hurt her and felt scared of being depressed again.

After the first session, she thought that she would have replied that she wanted to concentrate on current problems and find better ways of handling them, but now she wanted 'to understand why I feel this way'. Again, this reply is very encouraging to a psychoanalytic psychotherapist: she has learned that exploration is, overall, a good experience.

Assessment

My reaction to Charlie

I am struck at this point that Charlie is working hard and trying to be as honest and open as possible. She has presented a lot of potentially embarrassing material, and there are strong hints that she might be able to work in a psychodynamic/exploratory way.

In relation to her dream, she commented that looking after the cornet is 'an honour and a compliment'. In a similar way I feel that Charlie needs to know that the people she has trusted with this personal material have similar sensitivity and concern. I am also aware of the risk she is taking in giving access to such personal material, even though it is anonymous. Her potential for embarrassment and humiliation is probably being 'amplified' by me as a counter-transference reaction.

My feeling response is warm and positive towards her. I feel I can identify with her predicament, but I do not feel there is a significant risk of me becoming over-identified. I experience the common frustration of starting to feel engaged and to understand Charlie, while also being preoccupied with the inadequacy of the resources available to me. I am also thinking that in my NHS work I will need to bring things to a close and to prepare her to see someone else, who would actually take her on for therapy. Throughout the rest of this chapter, I will try to respond with both ways of working in mind: how I would work myself as a therapist, and some of the issues arising for a psychotherapist in the NHS, helping Charlie to find her way through the maze of therapeutic options.

'Listening' behind the words

The final step in gathering information is to 'listen with the third ear', which is obviously difficult with the constraint of not actually meeting Charlie! I decided to use a method drawn from my research and teaching interests to help develop this extra dimension. This involves going through a transcript and picking out hidden or unconscious meanings by focusing on the use of metaphors.

Ella Freeman Sharpe (1940) noticed that the 'dead metaphors' which fill everyday speech often carry partly concealed messages. Like Freud's concept of the 'compromise between a wish and a defence', the everyday habits of speech reveal areas of conflict. This allows me to mirror for Charlie the feared aspects of herself which are masked by her competent, coping self.

The list of metaphors was long (suggesting a richness to the material to be explored), but there was a focus on words like 'stuck', 'boring', 'burden', 'wasting'. A second theme was about sexuality, for example 'tarty', 'the curse', 'picked up'. Clearly, some metaphors are used consciously and others with less awareness. Here, I am not trying to find a 'correct' answer in the material, but trying to help myself to live imaginatively into Charlie's experience. I try to imagine what the raw experience of her childhood might have been. This is then linked with the words she used with most feeling. These are difficult to detect from a transcript, but I pick out 'feeble', 'unhappy', 'wasting' and 'control'.

I end up with a very powerful sense of Charlie as a child, which I can then develop and test out in our conversation to develop a 'shared feeling language'. I try to imagine Charlie as a young child. There are two parts: her depression seems to reflect an infant state of needing to be nursed, but feeling bored, feeble and helpless and most of all out of contact. My second 'imagined state' is later, when she feels controlled, humiliated and shamed, particularly about her emerging sexuality when she comes into conflict with an envious and unfulfilled mother.

Key issues in the material

Prior to drawing up a formulation of the problem, I need to mull over the material in a way which might initially seem unconnected but starts to cluster together as themes.

Early relationship with mother

I am struck by the description of an angry jerky quality to her movements. She is close to her feelings at times. She starts the session feeling ambivalent, and then focuses on mother, but tends to play down her own needs for therapy from very early on.

She focuses on mother's dominance and is aware that even when she is being assertive she is often still reacting to mother. There is a strong 'family myth' which is 'not to be questioned', which is later given 'scientific validity'. Charlie is aware that she would have been aborted and mother often refers to this. Why does mother say it even if it is true? Charlie often tries to empathize with mother but still feels hated. This is the start of a 'central dysfunctional belief' about herself as a worthless person.

Mother controls Charlie's appearance in great detail and often treats her as though she is a part of herself (although a loathed and hated part). There is evidence of continuing hate and envy in the story about the library books. She has to argue to herself that she is 'not that stupid'. There is also a strong suggestion of envy when

Charlie is going out and developing into a mature, sexual woman; and mother seems to see sexuality very negatively anyway, for example in the reference to periods. Mother's idiomatic use of 'you want to . . .' suggests a controlling presence. There is conflict about feeling that she could be valued if she were different from mother.

Charlie tends to turn against herself and hears her mother's internalized critical voice. She deals with this either by 'doing the opposite' or by identifying. There is a strong push/pull dynamic and she does not see the possibility of change. There is a strong inhibition of anger which might be directed towards the therapist at some point. She can identify with mother and this makes it less easy to express her anger towards her.

In the house she either cleans because mother tells her to or neglects it completely. This is perhaps true in her *internal* world also. She might keep things clean and orderly to keep at bay her angry, messy feelings under the mother's internalized 'look', or she can rebel. This leads her to accuse herself of being 'lazy', but is an important route to freedom from internal tyranny.

The lost child

She did not grieve for her own aborted child, and I wonder about the complex identifications that will be operating: her own identity as a mother, while feeling abandoned again by her own mother, and her identification with the damaged baby.

These are resonant themes and I link her presentation now with the ten-year anniversary. The unexpressed grief will probably be important in its own right, but will also link with the other key themes of identity, shame and loss. The theme of the lost child has been developed by David Doel (1992). He points out the parallel between an actual lost child and the psychological 'lost child': a regressed and repressed part of the self which needs to be integrated.

Formulation

This section draws together the foregoing threads into a more integrated formulation, which I will use with Charlie to plan the therapy.

Problems

Charlie feels her main problems to be: depression; feeling she lacks the courage of her convictions; feeling useless and inferior in relation to others. There is no serious character pathology, but pervasive difficulties in relationships (where she feels inferior and trapped) and also low self-esteem. There are difficulties in being open and trusting others.

There is conflict about autonomy and the expression of anger. She feels controlled, and deals with early feelings of rejection and emotional isolation by withdrawal and turning against herself. Nevertheless, there are some elements of a good sense of self which mainly show through her sense of autonomy in her job, her intelligence and her wry humour. She also experiences depression and depletion, although her coping style is generally good and she has not required any medical or psychological intervention.

She is fearful of damaging others. There seems to be a general rule: 'Being strong can damage others, being needy is bad'.

Reason for coming for therapy now

This might be the tenth anniversary of the abortion for which she has not grieved or it could be that her daughter is reaching the age when key conflicts regarding autonomy, worth and sexuality emerged in her own relationship with her mother.

Strengths

There is a strong side, including humour, psychological mindedness and acute observation of people. She feels strongly motivated and is able to weigh up the risks of therapy.

Core issues

As well as dealing with later issues of envy and rivalry with a dominant mother, Charlie is trying to deal with damage to her core sense of self. There may have been a problem with early self-object needs for admiration, which should have consolidated a strong sense of self. The core affect is of humiliation and embarrassment, which was later expressed in sexual put downs from her mother.

Internally, she lives in a world characterized by mother's envy of her own growth, intellect and sexuality and Charlie can only escape through 'identification with the aggressor'. In later life, she turns inward to avoid this aggressive part of her internal world from damaging others. Feeling comfortable with anger and aggression is an important developmental task. Charlie has no consistent experience of a loving relationship where she can at times be assertively angry. Instead, she has had to deal with the experience of being undermined and even her existence being denied. Mother's comments about wishing she had aborted Charlie, that she 'should have been a boy', and her scorn at Charlie's emerging sexuality mean that Charlie is faced with a dilemma: to become like her mother and take the risk of damaging others or to turn away.

The common escape route for a daughter is to have a strong relationship with a father who does not abuse his position by transgressing boundaries. This has not been possible for Charlie, and there is a need for a therapist (of either gender) to take on the necessary position. For Charlie, there is a price to be paid for this avoidance of her anger: there is an inhibition of her ability to be open and engaged with others; there is a diminished sense of her own effectiveness, and she is prone to depression because her anger is partly turned against herself.

The 'family myth' of her being a boy may serve a defensive function as well as being the expression of her mother's rejection of her as a separate woman. This has confirmed her lack of self-worth, but there does not seem to be any significant disturbance of gender identity.

One way of summarizing the formulation is in terms of a coexisting wish and fear. She wishes to be close, nurtured and valued, while fearing being humiliated and let down. There is a rule operating through Charlie's life: *If you are strong you may damage others, but if you are dependent on others you risk being despised.*

Therapeutic possibilities

The choice of therapy is in some ways straightforward for Charlie, in that she is psychologically minded, not too ill, and motivated to change. This means that she is likely to benefit from any type of therapy and so I would see my role as helping her to make an informed choice between the various options.

There is a conflict between the desire to give Charlie as much time as she might want, and attempting to provide a therapy of the 'right' length. This is a difficult concept to hold on to at times. It is more difficult for a therapist to work within a tightly defined focus towards goals which have been agreed with her than it would be to offer an empty canvas to explore issues in depth. Brief therapy is like a miniature painting: the work is detailed and precise, but there may be less space for full expression of some themes.

Charlie could almost certainly benefit from a group approach, but her own comments about maintaining a coping front would make this approach more difficult for her.

She is clearly psychologically minded, intelligent, is able to make connections and use metaphor. These characteristics are highly

favourable to a psychodynamic approach. She has considerable personal strengths and reasonable stability. The degree of depression is
not severe at the point of filling in the questionnaire, and there are
no real indications to consider non-psychotherapy alternatives such
as medication; but I would be thinking that part of my responsibility is to be open about the evidence on treatment effectiveness.

Here, unlike in severe depression, the situation is relatively easy,
in that the research evidence suggests that anti-depressant medication is no more effective than cognitive therapy or psychodynamic
therapy. There are no major contra-indications for psychotherapy
and so the decision will be made largely by discussion of preferences. In a way, the therapist here is like a travel agent: there are
several travel options but there is also an important choice about
how to travel to a given destination.

It is tempting to short-circuit the decision-making process. My
task is to help in weighing up the costs (not just financial but also
Charlie's time and energy) and risks against the benefits she can
expect. I will discuss this in the context of Charlie being broadly in
favour of an exploratory approach. The extent to which we could
work out an agreed focus would help us to decide between a short-
term approach and longer-term therapy.

For Charlie, psychodynamic therapy is likely to be relatively free
of risks. The usual risks of regression during the therapy, over-
dependence on the therapist and distraction from other key relationships need to be put to her, but I do not think there are any
additional risks here.

The course of therapy

Psychodynamic therapy would be a much easier therapy to offer if
it were possible to try a brief, focused approach first, and then extend it for a further year or two if the issue has not been resolved.
This is to fall into the drug paradigm of 'dosage' of therapy. In
practice, the different lengths of therapy need different styles: brief
therapy requiring much more activity to keep the focus and also an
early interpretation of transference material. In longer-term therapy,
I would be less active and expect a gradual development of a complex transference relationship within which the key relationship
themes will overlap in a complex way.

It may still be worthwhile to offer a trial period before making
a commitment to a long-term therapy. I make it explicit that the
therapy will only go ahead if we both feel happy with progress after
six weeks. This is, however, not the same as a brief therapy.

There is also a choice about frequency of therapy. My usual practice is weekly therapy, but many therapists would take the view that more frequent therapy (three times weekly or more) is necessary to develop the intensity of relationship which will allow fundamental change.

The early stage of the therapy will be tentative, with Charlie holding to a 'straightforward' view of what was happening; but gradually feelings from earlier relationships will come to the fore. This process is helped by having a very clear set of arrangements. Therapists from different persuasions sometimes feel that the strict adherence to the same time and place is an affectation. I would see the precision in these matters to be necessary. The close attention to detail will often allow us to focus on areas that might otherwise be lost. These will typically relate to the key themes already seen in the formulation of the problem.

Other than these general comments, the course of the therapy is difficult to predict, but my earlier comments on the likely themes say something about the terrain we might explore. There are likely to be times when Charlie feels distressed by memories, and other times where the focus will be on the experience of the relationship with me. The emphasis of my account has been on the early discussion and assessment because this provides a map for the therapy. However, the 'map' is not a route map: there is no clear path that I will steer, but the mapping we have done will allow me to recognize landmarks when they do appear.

The middle phase of therapy has endless variety, but the ending will probably reveal several common themes. There will be inevitable disappointment at what we have *not* accomplished and a return to the theme of loss. The therapy shifts its focus from the transference relationship to a more concrete sense of who we are and why we are there.

Problem areas

The move from assessment into therapy might be a point of difficulty in the work with Charlie. She will have experienced me as quite active with a lot of interventions to clarify and highlight what she is saying. In the therapy itself I will be more reflective, and there might be a pressure on me to avoid silences and any resulting tension in the session. I will have tried to prepare for this in the assessment phase, both by describing what might happen, and also by allowing the experience of silence. I will have tried several 'trial interpretations'. These are partly to check the accuracy of the tentative formulation and also to see how we might work with uncertainty. Robert Hobson has pointed out a paradox: it is in getting things optimally wrong that much progress is made.

The main area of difficulty for Charlie might be in experiencing the rage which has been held back for many years. I do not know at this point how it might come to the foreground. It might appear suddenly directed towards me for some apparently trivial error – being a few minutes late, anger at one of my mannerisms or habits of speech. Whatever the trigger, it is likely that I will have to stay with the experience for some time before understanding it.

Psychoanalytic psychotherapy requires an engagement between Charlie and her therapist which is both personal and professional. If that therapist is me, I have to face the possibility that Charlie may not find it easy to work with me. The opposite possibility is a significant risk in psychoanalytic psychotherapy: that Charlie might become over-reliant on me as a source of knowledge and nurturance. This is an intrinsic risk for any type of therapy, but there are no suggestions that the risks are particularly high for Charlie.

I wonder whether some particular transference themes might emerge. There is a theme in the material from the period she stayed in London as a child of 'finding out what makes things tick'. Perhaps this curiosity will occur with me, which could be positive, but could also be defensive.

There is a particular sensitivity to feeling that she has caused illness: I wonder what will happen if I become ill at some point in the therapy. The experience could allow Charlie to move on from her belief, but equally it could consolidate it.

Criteria for successful outcome

My general approach is to have different levels of objectives, agreed as far as possible with Charlie.

First level: These would refer to resolution of the symptoms which are currently causing difficulty. Here I would focus primarily on the features of depression. They will probably vary with time anyway, and are rather general and so of limited use.

Second level: These are the more specific issues, expressed in Charlie's own words. Here 'lacking the courage of my convictions' and 'feeling guilty about my mother' might be examples. These are much more difficult to pin down, but I would try as far as possible to link them to how she would know change had occurred.

The exercise might involve imagining life without these problems, and that exercise alone can be therapeutic. However, it is difficult to do this from a state of demoralization, and can seem crass and insensitive; after all, Charlie may well have come to see me because she cannot see a way through to the future.

These aims can only really be agreed with Charlie herself, but I imagine they would include some of the points she made about not apologizing to people, being more confident, and less reactive to others' needs. Also, we would try to see how her lessened guilt towards her mother would be shown, say, if she received a telephone call.

The combination of levels 1 and 2 is not particularly dependent on the model of therapy, although the choice of items might well be particularly focused on sense of identity, self-esteem and relationship issues in psychodynamic models.

The weakness of this approach is that it does not focus adequately on unconscious processes. There is no easy way round this, but the third level of assessing outcome, drawing from the work of David Malan (1979), tries to make some predictions based on psychodynamic theory.

Third level: There should be evidence that there has been a shift in Charlie's inner world. Her inner world is dominated by the power of her mother: this means the inner representation of mother. The inner voice of her mother should ideally be less harsh, or at least Charlie should feel less driven by guilt or the need for appeasement. This can be observed during the therapy, but there should be some external validation. Will Charlie be able to be assertive and angry without the fear of causing damage? Will this assertiveness be free of the quality of being 'reactive to mother'?

A good outcome would be for Charlie to have reduced depression, and more ability to be assertive in meeting her own needs, while being able to relate with increased depth and richness to close figures in her life. Perhaps I should state explicitly that one of my main aims is not to make Charlie's predicament worse. *Primum non nocere* (First, do no harm!) is one of the valuable residues of my medical training.

Summary

Charlie has a good chance of benefiting from psychoanalytic psychotherapy with relatively little risk. Other therapy models may be quicker at reducing some of the presenting symptoms but, given her strong preference for a psychodynamic way of working, I would feel happy to offer this. I would regret the need to end my contact after only an assessment in my NHS work.

There is always so much to explore and the length of this contribution means that I have highlighted some aspects of the material but neglected others. I would have liked to have spent more time on the name 'Charlie', which must mean a lot, but knowing it is a pseudonym I have played it down. Nevertheless, I am reminded of *The Well of Loneliness* by Radclyffe Hall (1928), a novel which explores the main theme of Charlie's story: a girl is born to a couple longing to have a son, and the child is called Stephen. Although the novel primarily deals with the issue of sexual identity, there is a telling section at the beginning where the mother's hate of her child is explored: 'But her eyes would look cold, though her voice might be gentle, and her hand when it fondled would be tentative, unwilling'.

The work on this chapter has highlighted for me the tension between working as a psychoanalytic therapist and my interest in research. For me, psychotherapy is always at the boundary between 'knowing about' a person and 'knowing' another person directly. At other times, the issue is to stay with the feeling of 'not knowing'.

The attempt to know something about Charlie has led me to experience this odd combination very directly. With limited information I feel confident about the likelihood that therapy will help and that the risks are modest, but I also feel some sense of knowing through an act of imagination which, like psychoanalytic therapy, is an intermingling of Charlie's world and of what I bring. There is also a vast sense of not knowing, of glimpsing another person, and feeling we have barely touched the surface. This is a painful, marginal experience, which characterizes the life of many therapists. It is particularly so where much of my work is taken up with brief meetings and, sadly, the meeting with Charlie has been more fleeting than most.

Further reading

Bowlby, J. (1979). *The Making and Breaking of Affectional Bonds*. London: Tavistock.

Casement, P. (1986). *On Learning from the Patient*. London: Tavistock.

Doel, D. (1992). The lost child and the Christ child. In *Out of Clouds and Darkness*. London: Unitarian Publications/Lindsey Press.

Hall, R. (1928). *The Well of Loneliness*. London: Jonathan Cape. (Reprinted 1982, London: Virago Press.)

Hobson, R.F. (1985). *Forms of Feeling: The Heart of Psychotherapy*. London: Tavistock.

Malan, D.H. (1979). *Individual Psychotherapy and the Science of Psycho-dynamics*. London: Butterworth.

Sharpe, E.F. (1940). An examination of metaphor: Psycho-physical problems revealed in language. *International Journal of Psychoanalysis*, Vol. 21, p. 201. (Reprinted in Fliess, R. (Ed.), *The Psychoanalytic Reader*. Madison, WI: International Universities Press.)

Stern, D.N. (1985). *The Interpersonal World of the Infant*. New York: Basic Books.

ALIX PIRANI

HUMANISTIC-TRANSPERSONAL PSYCHOTHERAPY

The therapist

My training in psychotherapy was not conventional, and I call myself a practitioner of humanistic/transpersonal psychology, or a body–mind–spirit therapist, to describe the perspectives and techniques clients might expect of me. After 25 years as a teacher of English literature and creative writing, I trained in the humanistic psychology tradition, which originated in America, and was then developing in Britain with limited resources. We were having to integrate a number of approaches, via short trainings, into coherent practice: a challenging and creative task which continues to this day. In 1980, I completed an Antioch MA in humanistic psychology and in 1993 was registered by the UKCP as a practitioner of humanistic and integrative psychotherapy.

The main therapies and techniques I experienced and have incorporated into my practice are creative therapies such as gestalt and psychodrama, and body–mind therapies, notably bioenergetics and primal regression – with a particular interest in the birth process – and most recently 'transpersonal counselling', which derives from psychosynthesis and Jungian approaches. The relationship between therapist and client is crucial, and here I was initially influenced by the views of Rogers and Buber, emphasizing the equality of persons in the interaction, unlike behavioural, analytic and psychiatric practice, which may reduce the client to an object or subject for observation. Study of Object Relations theory, especially Klein, Winnicott and Milner, helped me develop the transference/counter-transference relationship in the context of fostering creativity. While I have benefited from my reading in the wealth of analytic experience, and participation in analytic groupwork, my central aim is to enable clients to pursue their own development, with me as sounding-board, facilitator, guide, counsellor or whatever seems appropriate at the time – often a silent presence. In determining what a client might be experiencing, I find value in developmental approaches, both in ego psychology – notably Erikson's – and the transpersonal concern with life transitions. I seek to honour the soul in psycho-therapy: I believe that spiritual malaise is behind much of the dis-tress and sickness that is brought to us. The balancing of the 'masculine' and 'feminine' is central to creative sexuality and spir-ituality and informs all my work.

Increasingly, I find that sociopolitical factors must be taken into account as the context in which the client, and the therapy, exists (and suffers) in our present world; the impact on the individual of the conscious and unconscious collective must be acknowledged. Feminism has profoundly affected my outlook; feminist therapy theory, and especially the work of the Jungians Perera and Woodman, has influenced my work with women, and with creativity generally. Family and group therapies, and awareness of race and class issues, provide valuable perspectives on what may be determining a client's behaviours and roles in life.

Integrating all these viewpoints and practices continues as I aim to be a whole therapist working with the whole person. My writing is part of that endeavour: the published work most relevant to Charlie's situation is cited at the end of this chapter.

Further information requested

Here are the further questions I requested be put to Charlie, together with her verbatim answers or my summary of her response:

How would she feel about having therapy from a woman?
Authoritative women tend to make her feel inhibited: she's more comfortable with men in a position of authority.

Can she report any particular dream(s), recent or from the past?
I dreamed about my daughter's cornet on Sunday. She'd
given it to me to look after, and I'd lost it. And I was trying
desperately to find it, and I couldn't. And it was such a relief
when I woke up. She's only just started cornet – this is my
youngest daughter, the nine-year-old . . . and she loves it. She
takes her cornet to bed with her. The fact that she then

trusted it to me in my dream was quite an honour and a compliment, so it was a relief when I woke up. Other than that – I don't remember many dreams to be honest.

Are there any she'd rather not describe?
Yes. I used to have a recurring dream with very obvious sexual imagery, when I was in my teens, and it always ended the same way. Just even thinking about it frightens me. To describe it would be really difficult.

Does she n/ever get depressed?
You mean seriously depressed – like clinical depression? Well yes, since I was about 13, 14, I've had spells of – well, I describe it as depression: it's just total hopelessness, and thinking that I'll never be happy again. And becoming completely apathetic, and I don't sleep well. And feeling that it will always be like this . . .

If so, why did she not mention it in her interview?
I think because when I'm not depressed I try to pretend that – you see I think of it as a cloud, that never actually goes away – it just sort of goes up and down. And when it's up and I'm out of it, then that's all right. But one day it will come back. And I try not to tempt providence by talking about it when I'm not feeling particularly depressed. I mean when I came last year I was a bit unhappy about a lot of things, but I wasn't what I would describe as depressed.

Did she suffer post-natal depression?
No, post-natal euphoria was more my sort of thing.

What does she generally feel about her body and health at present?
She feels very healthy at present. She gave up smoking a year ago.

What is she most afraid of at this stage of her life? Is she aware of the menopause approaching? How does she view this prospect? How does she feel about her mother's ageing process?
She fears that when her children leave she'll have ageing grandparents to care for. She realizes she is ageing herself. Though not especially afraid of the menopause to come, she is frightened of any return of a very severe depression in which she feels self-destructive and near-suicidal. Fending it off is the daunting prospect.

Does she know anything about her own birth? If not, would her mother be likely to offer details? Could she ask her, and report back to M.J.?
I was actually born in my grandmother's house, just before the ambulance came. I would probably ask – I don't know why I haven't asked whether I was breastfed because she's seen me breastfeed my own . . . I know quite a bit about my birth. It's a family joke. I gather that she wasn't really all that aware of what to expect. She woke up early in the morning about six with what she thought was wind, and she went down – we had an outside toilet . . . eventually about quarter to seven my grandmother came down and said, 'You've been down here a long time', and my mum said, 'Yes, I've got this terrible wind, it's sort of coming and going'. By the time the ambulance came I'd come already, and my grandmother apparently found some sheets to put on the living room floor, discovered they were her very best sheets, and took them away again, and then found some other sheets which were pretty messy by the time the ambulancemen arrived. Everybody teases me that I was in such a hurry to get there. Two hours is pretty short.

What has been her relationship with, and feeling about, her sister, from the time she was born and up until now?
Charlie speaks at length of her present lukewarm relationship with her sister Mary: 'My sister is very like my mother and I'm very different from both of them'. She is caught in a triangle here, but she ignores the crucial question of how she felt when her sister was born. She speaks disapprovingly of Mary's extravagant ideas and coldness as a mother.

How old was she when she married?
Two weeks after my twenty-fifth birthday.

What is her husband's age now?
He's younger than me – thirty-nine.

Does she feel she's happily married?
Yes . . . I am.

Can we have a family tree, with her comments?
Charlie provided a five-generation family tree with accompanying comments as to who was particularly significant to her: these were asterisked. I noted: (1) that family members were and still are more in contact than is common these days, and there is a strong extended

family feeling; (2) that the women in particular were asterisked and remarked on; (3) that several men who were important died young – including two 'heroes' not on the tree: 'Both died fighting Fascism and hence their heroic status in the family'; (4) that on her mother's side a powerful Welsh consciousness is carried by the women, one of whom was given the name of a dark Celtic witch: 'wind-hag and vampire'; (5) that probably the most powerful woman in Charlie's background, her maternal grandmother, is not asterisked.

What is her relationship to the Church, and to religion (cf. visit to St Paul's)? Does her Trades Union involvement have any similarity of commitment?

Yes, it's strange that really. I was brought up in the Church of England, and my grandmother in particular was extremely religious. [She goes on to describe her involvement in the church choir and youth club, her feelings of attraction to atmosphere and ritual, and attending a Roman Catholic Mass, which affected her strongly]: And I thought, it's almost like . . . well, not being drugged, it's that hypnotic kind of thing, and it's never really meant anything. So I stopped going, and neither of us are particularly religious. I wouldn't say that I was anti-religious . . . A lot of people say that Socialism is my religion . . . I think, yes, you get a kind of . . . well, I don't know . . . I don't think I've ever had a religious experience like that, but certainly in terms of devotion and belief in a set of principles, yes it is my replacement if you like.

How does she react to what's going on internationally and nationally?

[Charlie's conscience and humanity is much challenged by the painful events in Bosnia. Of the situation in Britain]: . . . this government is so incompetent. But ever since 1979 people like me have been on the wrong side, if you like, and I accept that that is how it's going to be for the foreseeable future. I mean, with every election that Labour has lost I've got more and more demoralized. Yes, things are just so awful.

What are her feelings about, and expectations of, her children (each individually)?

Her answers on her three children James, Rosalind and Alanna, given in vivid detail and at length, are of interest in revealing aspects of her own personality reflected in them. She is a thoughtful, attentive and loving mother, genuinely interested in her children's very different personalities, proud of them, concerned and anxious, careful not to expect too much of them, nor to be as inflexible as her own mother. There is a strong feeling of unease – 'Where did I go wrong?' – particularly in relation to the oldest, James. Nothing is said about the father's role in his, or in the daughters', development.

Are they a happy family?
I hope we are. We have rows. Sometimes . . . well normally we have rows with Rosalind. And they can be shattering. She can slam doors so hard that the house shakes. But, yes on the whole we are.

Does the family ever make her feel inadequate, in the way her mother has?
No. I make myself feel that way I think, but they don't. No.

Are there any feelings she can't express in the family?
You mean openly to them? No, I don't think so. Particularly as the older two have got older, we've tended to talk about our feelings fairly openly.

She goes on to describe how her ambivalent, painful feelings about her abortion were shared and discussed with the children, at the time and subsequently; clearly their openly expressed reactions, and understanding, helped to heal her distress.

Where and when does she get most happiness and pleasure in her life?
Oh . . . with the children, when they're all . . . not being good, when they're not going out of their way to upset me. With my husband. With my friend. With friends I've had in the past as well. I suppose my ideal evening is spent at home with a few really close friends who I know well, and the children as well, now they're older. With the kind of music I like. And if I have to be on my own, with a few good books, that sort of thing: that's paradise to me!

I also put some questions to M.J., for further information about her presence.

When you're with Charlie, what emotional age do you feel she is?
Fifteen in some ways, although my first [unthought out] response was thirteen and then seventeen to your question, so perhaps I am striking a balance in coming down on fifteen!

Is she uncomfortable in her body?
   She moves her hands a lot, expressively but also nervously.
   Bitten fingernails. But I'd say more 'gangly' at times than
   awkward or uncomfortable.

What is her eye contact like?
   Looks away quite a lot, but I find this quite normal in
   someone who is really thinking about what she wants to say,
   or really gets into what she is saying. She looks at me when
   I speak with her.

*Her breathing? My impression so far is that it's anxious, but maybe that
was initial nervousness.*
   I don't notice this as marked in any way. She is anxious, but
   I don't think it is initial nervousness.

Is there any very marked effect she has on you?
   She makes me feel a bit anxious, as though it's difficult for
   her to feel relaxed with me; although I find her openness,
   her thoughtfulness, her sense of humour (sometimes at her
   own expense) and her enthusiasm for thinking about the
   questions is very engaging, and I would much enjoy working
   with her were I the therapist.

M.J.'s reactions gave me the impression that Charlie's anxiety is
infectious and perhaps controlling. She came across as a teenager, so
there may have been sexual unease; but I suspect there was an
infant there, afraid she will not get what she needs, which makes
parents and foster-parents anxious that they cannot satisfy her.

Assessment

I think Charlie is at a stage of radical transformation of which she
is only partially aware. Her body and emotions are registering the
fear–awe–excitement–depression that mark the surfacing of unconscious material. She is forty-two, one of the seven-year life passages
and, for a woman, the beginning of the pre-menopausal years. Her
fatalistic sense of being inescapably 'cursed' by a bad mother vies
with her wish to be freed from her so as to make independent
meaning of the rest of her life. I see this as a mid-life crisis.
   Charlie's feelings of 'unwantedness' and low self-esteem have
immediacy, as does a fierce instinctive belief in her own worth. Her
entry into the project recalls her soul's initial decision to enter the

uncertain womb: 'I had second thoughts about coming in case I was wasting your time'. She has known also the power of her defiance but is less aware of her power as a victim to manipulate authority. Though the womb and perhaps the breast was unwilling and depriving, she survived, with a will to live and the strong constitution of her mother's side of the family, having fortunately not inherited the paternal congenital weakness. She always survives, but with the constant anxiety that she won't, a fear of failure of resources – which often means insufficient breath. She seems to live off her nerves and her own fat: thin and 'gangly', loquacious, ungrounded, not expecting to be heard, seen, fed, appreciated – keeping relationships going with her attractive high energy and open, sometimes violent, expressiveness. She has to hold herself together and isn't quite substantial enough to do that. Along with her constricted breathing, her heart is often painfully closed – this is the apathy in her depression.

Charlie's energy works on 'deficiency motivation'. It has very marked class and social correlations. Her family history is very representative of material and cultural changes in British life during this century. Part of her need is to discover a new identity which goes beyond the one established for women in earlier contexts. Her body and feelings are using outworn political mechanisms, and she is bewildered by the relationship between the masculine and the feminine in her own roles, energies, psyche – and in the practical 'political' and moral issues her children present her with.

The dream of Alanna and the cornet contains some of this bewilderment, in the immediate context: her realization of a deep nightmare fear of losing, which can only be dealt with by a flight into wakefulness (this reflects her manic way of avoiding depression). The nightmare is of her own inner little girl's loss of the potent harmonizing male – the man out there or the masculine within, in the context of mother's untrustworthiness and inability to hold him, or the masculine principle, for her. Possibly, prior to the meeting with M.J., there were feelings about the eventual loss of his paternal care. Alanna's anger, and her own, cannot be faced.

Loss and inadequate mourning characterize Charlie's development. There is repeated evasive denial of loss and abandonment, and suppression of anger and grief; especially by her mother, whose bereavements resulted in guilt-feelings, denial of vanished joy, bitterness and gritty determination to survive. Charlie could not show her own deep pain and heartbreak, nor mourn at depth – only with unmet surface weeping – when threatened by loss of the womb, the breast, mother when hospitalized with whooping-cough, mother when sister was born soon after, then father. . . . The five-year-old learned to 'put it all behind her' and pretend it had not upset her much. Puritanical martyrdom and working-class heroism were her mother's way of coping and surviving: it was part of the infant's cultural training, as Erikson (1965) would bear out.

I note also the anal compulsiveness of Charlie's mother, and of the grandmother, whose unmentioned death occurred just prior to Charlie's puberty and first severe depression. She wouldn't let her be born onto her nice clean sheets. Charlie must have felt like an objectionable object, a piece of shit, even nearly born into a lavatory. Her toilet-training would have coincided with the three major losses of her early life.

This found its way into her adolescence. Anal and sexual control were still confused, menstruation treated with disgust. Her adolescence was never satisfactorily completed. She feels she lacks mature adult identity as a woman, and her feminine presence is that of a girl 'either thirteen or seventeen', two crucial stages in her own life, now being recalled as she sees them in her children: the firstborn lacking confidence, the second full of irrepressible sexual vitality.

As she suspects, the internalized 'bad mother' has been at work here. It is surely the envious mother. She must have envied her firstborn – a wanted boy, who had a father, and competed with her perhaps for father's attention, as doubtless does the shameless Rosalind.

Envy is a major dynamic in her emotional scenario: envy by her mother of her life, and her own of her sister's. According to Klein's understanding of the nature of envy, her behaviour even now is paranoid-schizoid, and she is struggling through the depressive position without help (Segal 1979). She could not work through this in her teens, with her mother still the sole providing breast: envious, poisonous, driven further into that state by Charlie's projections. The absence of a dependable father who could help her stand up to mother, and could validate her sexuality in a safe way, has left her with insecurity and fear of her own uncontainable energy, her womanpower. This presumably was manifest in the recurring unmentionable dream.

The absent father, though idealized as hero, has a hidden negative face – he too gave her life and then abandoned her. Doubtless the gaze of the sickening man seemed – was – envious of her very being.

The sense of her life being threatened has deeper spiritual implications, at this stage of questioning the meaning of her existence – of everyone's. There is a male God whose church seems empty to her, and he was envious too – of the matriarchy he suppressed, turning spiritually powerful women into witches. This matriarchy is doubtless in the Celtic tradition Charlie comes from, which can be a vital source of strength; roots which, like her working-class roots, need to be explored and honoured – the loss of what is irretrievable in them mourned, and their positive surviving strengths reclaimed. She needs to contact the 'women's mysteries' of that tradition, which should be taught after puberty, when sexual/spiritual power is developing. Instead, the power to 'bewitch' is suppressed and the loving becomes hating.

The accumulation of such negative power hooks into the archetype: the obsessive nature of Charlie's feelings suggests that the 'dark goddess', the destructive Mother, has taken hold of Charlie's psyche. She needs to acknowledge its presence and cease to be unawarely driven by it. It may be demanding of her that she right its wrongs. With characteristic feminine psychic sensitivity, she is connecting with what is happening in the collective. In the immediate collective context, I imagine Margaret Thatcher has been a similarly threatening figure for Charlie over the past years, making her despair and lose hope in the socialism which is her patriarchal religion.

Success and failure in the eyes of others matters greatly to Charlie; performance anxiety threatens to undermine her outer self-confidence. This must have origins in her confused toilet-training. Language development is coincident with that stage: control of the two orifices runs in parallel, and Charlie's disturbed patterns of silence and protest are still evident. There is a recurring situation: her grandmother, mother, she herself and her daughter are all between two and three and a half when a younger sister arrives to disturb this crucial phase in which autonomy develops – or doesn't. Grandmother dictates the rules, and each girl loses her battle for autonomy – the battle now enjoined between Rosalind and Charlie.

Mother's power in the triangle is divisive: she plays the sisters off against one another. Charlie expects little of her relationship with Mary and fears her own well-being has somehow cursed her sister's health. But the competitiveness is unacknowledged and there seems scant allegiance in the face of the controlling mother. This weakens Charlie's sense of herself as a woman: our sisters are our mirrors and co-creators.

Charlie presents herself as an unwanted child (unwanted sister?) but I believe that may be more of a self-fulfilling myth than the whole truth. She has 'basic trust', a capacity to love herself, inspire love and be joyful with friends and family. Her first years with her youthful parents were possibly lighthearted ones in which she was enjoyed for who she was, once she'd arrived. Grandmother provided a home. But her mother doubtless felt she was being punished for her sexual transgression by Charlie's illness and her husband's death; she became guilt-ridden and bitter – the blessing of the baby was erased from memory and Charlie became a burden to curse her. There is a strong mythic feeling here: the Garden of Eden, lost innocence, Eve's sinfulness and fall from grace. It is good to know that Charlie can now talk of evenings at home with the people, music and books she loves as 'paradise'.

Therapeutic possibilities

Could I be successful with this client? This begs the question of 'success' and 'failure' – one of Charlie's issues. And it seems to imply 'cure', so there is a danger too that she may be regarded as more unhealthy than she is, and more acceptable when ill than well. So when I ask myself 'does she really need therapy?', I know that 'therapy' must remain undefined except as a process of finding out what her needs are. I can only consider how well we might do that. Charlie's qualities suggest she can make good use of therapy and her therapist: insight, flexibility, 'basic trust', a readiness to learn well, and the capacity to play, which, as Winnicott (1971) affirms, is vital. I think she has the ego-strength to go into depression and the night-mare breakdown she fears, if need be with the understanding and support of those around her, as well as mine. Her occasional feelings of craziness are, as far as I can judge, containable, once they are accepted as inevitable disorientations experienced especially by women in a crazy-making world. Such feelings can be grounded, physically and philosophically. The depression I see as, at its deep-est, a transitional 'dark night of the soul'; the near-suicidal feelings are her crucial encounter with mortality, where she makes her own choice to live – to want the birth of her emerging self even if others do not want it or her. Though Charlie does not somatize her distress in obvious illness, I suspect her anxiety is caused by traumatized breathing, originating possibly at birth but then drastically with the near-fatal whooping cough: voice-control is erratic, and she could benefit from work on the 'dis-ease' of her throat and lungs. This has doubtless been masked by the smoking she has courageously given up: the addiction to harmful suffocating cigarettes overcome, she now can deal with the addiction to the harmful suffocating mother.

So, speaking now as Charlie's adoptive therapist, my initial con-cern is to help her keep breathing and ground her fears and angers in her body and her matter-of-fact world, while her unconscious does the 'upsetting' it needs to do to transform her life, allowing the old personality to die and a new one to be born. My own ground here is that I have experienced such transitions myself, and survived loss of faith, sanity and identity: I trust this process. In the 'matter-of-fact' world, I am a mother and grandmother, and have been through many of the emotional disruptions caused by social mobility and cultural dislocation. I too was unwanted, and an attempt to abort me failed. I am one of two sisters. I have learned much about my own role as victim and how we women find a negative power through that.

In all this I feel an ally of Charlie's. However, I know that, being roughly the same age as her mother, I'm probably going to be taking some powerful projections. At the negative end, these could range from intellectual manipulation, through emotional onslaught and humiliation, to possibly profound annihilative psychic attacks. I cannot predict that, and certainly will not be misled into inciting it, but on past experience I trust I can take it if need be. Charlie's sense of humour, and mine, will be invaluable in dealing with this kind of scenario; I think we share some sense of the irony of life. And as I believe such an interaction is between only certain aspects or 'sub-personalities' of two persons, I would make sure not to neglect the creative connections between our energies, which are less highly charged, less intense.

The unknowns which may affect the 'success' of the work, limiting my power to facilitate the process as I would hope to, are Charlie's husband and family, and how far she is inescapably part of their process and may choose to subordinate her needs to theirs. Such a choice could be a regrettable retrogression to her negative patterns of self-denial and martyrdom, or it could be a conscious positive decision to make a sacrifice and accept 'delayed gratification' for the common family welfare which means so much to her. As yet her husband is scarcely visible, perhaps concealed and protected. Not surprisingly, as I am already aware of how easily I can slip into her mother's place of envying Charlie's marriage to him and their happy flourishing family, and wanting to undermine his influence with her, for fear of being discarded myself. I trust I do not have too much ego-investment in being the indispensable omniscient therapist, and can leave the next generation to lead their own lives according to their own criteria of fulfilment. Pathology-oriented therapy can erode people's confidence: therapists often put their own depression on their clients. I hope my internal and external supervisors will prevent me from doing that.

The course of therapy

I think Charlie and I have had the equivalent of the initial interview I usually arrange. Thereafter, if she wishes, we meet for four sessions, then have a review and a decision whether to proceed – either of us can withdraw if we wish, without overmuch explanation – though I do take care, from my position of responsibility, not to leave someone feeling hurtfully rejected. It is unlikely I would want not to continue with Charlie unless something unsuspected is revealed which changes my mind (e.g. that she has worked her way through half a dozen therapists in the past couple of years!).

We meet once a week for one hour. The agreed fee is paid at the time; it is also due if the client misses the session without twenty-four hours' notice. I ask that termination of therapy be agreed between us at a fixed date arranged well in advance, preferably one month for every year it has lasted. How long it will last I cannot say: 'It takes as long as it takes'. My guess for Charlie is from one to three years, depending on all kinds of factors, and I hope she is prepared to contemplate that possibility – she will of course decide as we go along.

The first four meetings are a kind of trial run in which we find out how we collaborate. I will mostly allow it to float, to see how Charlie communicates: her rhythms and energies, verbal and non-verbal, and what effect they have on me. I will offer occasional tentative observations and feedback, a taster of various techniques, like dream-exploration, body-awareness, role-play. I will also ensure she has a clear idea of the process we are embarking on, and that our own interaction is central; we will find that her relationships, past and present, will reproduce themselves in ours, can be observed and remoulded for the future.

If she agrees to continue, we will begin with what is uppermost, the 'top layer' of immediate concerns – feelings about her mother, some incident at work or at home, a dream. Important persons will be confronted through role-play or 'empty chair' work, and we will observe any difficulty in doing that. The aim is to focus, and not evade the truth. Fear can be explored verbally, and if it becomes so overpowering as to paralyse our progress, then discharged physically through shuddering while securely grounded. Dreams, language and events will begin to yield clues as to what is waiting to be communicated about the present or brought to memory from the past.

As I observe all this, I have my diagnostic hypotheses in mind, which I will be testing, but listening primarily to what she reveals to me – important for Charlie, who from an early age had to swallow the words and beliefs of others. We need to discover how significant awareness is erased, acted out, locked into the body and mind now – so I pay attention to process rather than to content. For example, if there is depression, we try to identify its reactiveness to events past and present, and the suppressed emotions it carries; but chiefly we discover how it is held in her body, mind and feelings in my presence. We accept too that it has its own unknowable meaning, which will emerge in time: our awe before that is vital.

Monitoring the process involves having a model to provide a map in time – just as the 'diagnosis' offers a map in space. A model of the therapeutic process must be one the therapist trusts; there are many I bear in mind, with roughly similar patterns. To oversimplify: for non-psychotic states, building up and breaking down, dying of the old personality, ego-lessness or 'chaos', re-birth, re-integration and formation of the new personality. I have long used the birth process as a model which is so ingrained in our inner creative experience that it reverberates at all awareness levels. For mothers in particular – therapists and clients – it has powerful resonances. However, this may not be a symbol that is current for Charlie; other symbols may appear in her language or dreams which accommodate her sense of direction. Charlie's language is relatively lacking in metaphor and she forgets her dreams; in her language development there was too much control, not enough poems and stories perhaps to give form to her babble – except grandfather's politically correct fairy tales! I will encourage her dream-life, fantasy world, drawing, free writing, as a way of stimulating her right-brain 'feminine' side and helping her cultivate the richness of her unique imagination. I can offer her the metaphor of birth as I might tell a story to a child. Other stories and myths could serve her, particularly that of Erishkegal and Inanna (explored by Perera 1981), the 'dark' and 'light' sister goddesses who confront one another in the underworld. This might reproduce itself in the therapy-room between us. And Demeter and Persephone are often there in the interaction between an older and younger woman.

It seems that at present sexuality and the inner and outer balance of masculine and feminine, male and female roles, mother and father, is a highly charged concern. The desire for 'conjunctio' is basic to everyone's psychic and biological need to create anew, and integrate. We will explore the dream of Alanna who has lost the cornet she takes to bed with her, and the earlier shocking dreams, and any sexual fantasies, examining their personal content and psychic symbolism.

Overshadowing the sexual scene is the mother who controls her sexually, even now wanting to cut off her hair, and who in old age will make further demands on her vital energy. Here is the archetypal crone, vampire even, whose waning sexuality and odour of decay lures and threatens and whose wisdom is often unwelcome. Charlie might see that in me. It would be another confrontation with Erishkegal, or Kali, Medusa, Lilith . . . the mother who gives life but may kill you also, the mother who aborts, or suffocates. To refer to my birth model: the 'conjunctio', however hard to accept, has to happen for the conception. Then later, after the exit from the 'paradisal' foetal existence through the gateway of the terrifying mother who casts you into nothingness, the establishment of the new life begins on the ground provided by the nursing mother, and others. Then it is the bisexual principle again that is important, the 'conjunctio' that brings right- and left-brain activity into balance to foster learning and create the newly developing self. Here is the benign, tender feminine archetype with a different wisdom: Inanna, Mary, Sophia. And putting these two 'opposites' together is similar activity, as the child learns that the mother who hates and the mother who loves is one and the same. At the moment, Charlie needs to sort this out first: to be sure of the safety and 'goodness' of the ground she will land on once she is born; to know I will be solid enough ground to appreciate her need to be an adult sexual/ creative woman, before she risks going back with me into the darker realms of mother's womb and terrifying absence. Using her own image, to be sure that I – and she – will not lose for her the cornet which is being learned, which is both a male and female symbol: a masculine, active vocal medium for the receptive feminine spirituality of music. I hope in reality she will learn to play an instrument or practise some other art form herself, and not leave it to her daughter to carry for her that medium of experimental truth-seeking, a 'transitional object' (see Winnicott 1971), lest that lead to Alanna having to perform correctly to suit her mother.

The ending of Charlie's therapy will be a crucial passage, since her past experiences of loss and leaving home are bound to be restimulated by the impending 'point of departure'. Our aim will be to see how it might be different this time, as we find her reacting to it as she did on previous occasions. Maybe she will take me by surprise, as she did with her mother at birth – so I cannot predict what will happen or how I will be left. I shall certainly spend time looking with her at how she will manage her life in the world outside mother's domain and continue on her own with the processes of integration we have learned together; and we will review the therapy and see what she feels she has gained and failed to gain from it. One of the most difficult aspects of this transition is going out into a world where the language, values and ways of being inherent in the therapeutic process, are alien and misunderstood. And that is exactly what Charlie, and so many of us, experienced in infancy. The romantics, Blake and Wordsworth, knew that only too well.

Problem areas

The problems I foresee, some of which I have already indicated, are ones which I feel would be 'solved' by the therapy itself – even having to deal with its failures. Disruption would probably be by external events: unexpected crises which might interrupt Charlie's commitment to the therapy, or my ability to support her. But there could be pressures, and deliberate or unconscious interference by friends or members of her family, where she might find herself trapped in a role which includes her being the 'referred patient' or the one who takes on the burden of solving the family's problems through therapy. In that case I would advise family or, if relevant, marital therapy with other therapists. For however much she and I might study the relationships in her family and what they reveal of aspects of herself – a woman's main identity being inevitably determined by her close involvement with her husband and children – we need to avoid the female 'matronizing' omnipotence which prevents men and children taking on the responsibility for emotional development themselves.

This kind of collusion is a problem that can develop when women are working together. There can be too much energy of a closed-circuit kind, reproducing the mother–daughter chain or sister impasse Charlie has been caught in. This could clear itself in relation to her real mother and sister, but there is the danger that I might unwittingly replace one mode of control with another and be blind to Charlie's needs, since it is part of her pattern to conceal her needs. I would certainly want a male supervisor to oversee this therapy. However, if I try to keep before us the question 'What does Charlie's soul need?', then 'control', and 'power over', should cease to be an issue – there can only be an essential heart connection.

One area in which I could become over-identified with Charlie is in that of the family and marriage, for it was when I was her present age that my marriage broke down and with it the family structure, our children then being of similar age to hers. The outcome of that is rebounding on us all twenty years later, and doubtless colours my view of her situation. The statistics of marriage breakdown these days inevitably make any intelligent parent anxious. The world soul, the *anima mundi*, is deeply troubled at present, and in so far as Charlie is a troubled soul, there are difficult times ahead. There is not a solution, there is only moving on, keeping the breathing, the spirit, going. To quote James Hillman (1983): 'The soul's eternal wanting is psychotherapy's eternal question'.

Criteria for successful outcome

I would hope to see Charlie emerge much more in charge of herself in emotional relationships and in her family, less of a helpless victim to her mother's criticisms and her own self-denigration and masochism. I hope she would be more balanced in her expectations and able to bring her managerial self-confidence to her feeling life. She will have gone through a necessary phase of disillusion to achieve realistic ambivalence, really owning the shadow in herself and in others, rather than apologetically thinking herself a failure, her mother all bad and men unreachable. The idealized 'goodness' that goes with romanticized or politicized heroism will need to be seen for the snare it is. And any idea that something (the therapy?) will one day magically heal her wounded self will need replacing with the acceptance that she may have to cease laying blame, however justified, on those who harmed her; live with the wound; and to discover what meaning it gives to her life. In time she may forgive her mother and father; maybe not.

I would expect all this to be manifest in a decrease of anxiety, the capacity to be more in repose and at peace with herself, with her frustrations and angers expressed wherever possible in the direction where they belong – her talking will then be less hysterical and nervous, and there should be an end to the inner dialogue with her mother, and an ability to speak with her in an open adult way. Her relationships with women generally should improve.

I would want to see Charlie better able to handle her depression when it comes upon her, accepting it as inevitable, be it a temporary mood, a seasonal need for hibernation, a retreat from unwelcome feelings that could be expressed, or the psyche's more radical need for oblivion. Avoidance only makes it worse. Its meaning emerges in time.

Opposite to the contracted state of depression is the expansion of Charlie's imaginative horizons: she should be taking more space for herself and her creativity, lest she lose all her creative vitality to her family and have none left when she arrives at the next seven-year passage and the nest is empty. Her schooling seems not to have encouraged her that much, but it is never too late to start again from scratch. She can contact powerful resources within herself.

Summary

In what I have written I am most aware of how difficult it is to convey what a therapeutic interaction is like, and since I have not met Charlie I feel I may be abusing her in some way by making interpretations at a distance. An experienced therapist becomes finely tuned to her client's rhythms, breathing, body language, silences, memories – her 'aura' – and even a verbatim account of a session could not convey these vital subtleties, nor what goes on in the intervals between meetings. As I see it, a therapy session, or series of sessions, is a poetic drama which my client and I – and the gods – play out together at a particular moment in time. There are possible scripts, an awareness of other texts, a great deal of improvisation, and hours of formlessness, stasis and boredom. These are not dramas meant for a public performance. Offering my imagined relationship with Charlie to the reader feels like a betrayal of the essential nature of therapy. So, instead, I offer it up to the gods, and wish Charlie well on her journey.

Further reading

Erikson, E. (1965). *Childhood and Society*. London: Penguin.
Hillman, J. (1983). *Healing Fiction*. New York: Station Hill Press.
Keleman, S. (1975). *Your Body Speaks its Mind*. New York: Simon and Schuster.
Perera, S.B. (1981). *Descent to the Goddess*. Toronto: Inner City Books.
Pirani, A. (1989). *The Absent Father*. London: Penguin Arkana.
Segal, H. (1979). *Klein*. London: Fontana/Collins.
Winnicott, D.W. (1971). *Playing and Reality*. London: Tavistock/Routledge.

ANTHONY RYLE

COGNITIVE-ANALYTIC THERAPY

The therapist

Until my retirement, I was probably the least trained consultant psychotherapist in the UK. For this reason, I cannot describe my therapeutic orientation in terms of allegiance to any of the established schools or training institutes. The best introduction will be to give an autobiographical account of my evolution as a therapist.

My first twelve years after qualifying in medicine were spent in a group general practice in North London, and it was there that I slowly discovered that I was more interested in the people and their lives than their illnesses. After a few years I became involved in research, first studying the prevalence of psychiatric disorders in my practice patients, and then investigating the relationship between the psychological health of children of primary school age and the emotional stability and marital relationships of their parents. This work demonstrated the high prevalence of untreated psychological distress in the population and taught me a lot about families, a process helped by working with an experienced social worker (Madge Hamilton) on the family study.

By this time I had begun to offer patients 'long appointments' outside surgery hours, and I worked several hours each week in a hospital outpatient department getting a lot of experience and a small amount of supervision for my psychotherapy. In order to extend my involvement in therapy, I left general practice in order to run a university health service, in which context such work was the central concern. Here I continued my research interest, again finding a high level of emotional and psychiatric disorder, and beginning to investigate the nature and extent of change produced by therapy.

The main instruments I used were versions of Kelly's repertory grid, a simple but powerful way of getting people to describe how they see themselves, and others and their relationships. Meanwhile, my psychotherapy experience grew, seeing patients in once-weekly therapy in most cases, but carrying a few more intensive and long-term cases. I was by now reading widely in the psychoanalytic literature, liking in particular the Object Relations approach of Guntrip and Winnicott, and I was in twice-weekly supervision (by the late Dr F. Shadforth) in a Freudian/Kleinian mode. This was supplemented by attending courses and by doing the introductory year and one further year at the Institute of Group Analysis.

The combination of reading more widely, of using a 'cognitive' research tool, and receiving psychoanalytic supervision, while remaining unhappy about many aspects of psychoanalytic theory and practice, led me to an increasing interest in integrating ideas and methods from different schools; this coincided with a similar growth in integrative approaches, especially in the USA. In particular, I wanted to incorporate Kelly's ideas and the cognitive-behavioural methods which research was showing to be effective, while retaining, but re-stating in a more cognitive language, the core of valuable understandings about personality development and about the therapeutic relationship which psychoanalysis had contributed.

This interest, growing through the 1970s, led finally to the evolution of a specific therapy, which was later labelled 'cognitive-analytic therapy' (CAT). In this, the various preoccupations of the three previous decades were drawn together.

Cognitive-analytic therapy was intended to be a treatment which could be supplied in the National Health Service (NHS), in that it was time-limited (usually 12–16 sessions) and applicable to a wide range of problems. Linked with this, it is an active therapy; sixteen sessions with a 25-year-old patient equals 0.000073 of the life so far, and to change the patterns of belief and behaviour developed over that life must involve work of high intensity from both patient and therapist. To be effective, this work must be well directed, and for that reason CAT is focused. But being focused does not imply being limited to selected or less severe problems. The key element in CAT practice is the joint work done in the early sessions, through which the patient's history is re-examined and his or her current ways of proceeding are described. These patterns of belief, feeling and acting, derived from early experience, and now causing damage and restriction, are seen to be self-maintaining in certain ways (see the 'Psychotherapy File' below). The core of the therapy is to help the patient first recognize and then consciously revise them. This is achieved by self-monitoring in daily life, by noting their manifestation in the therapy relationship and by the therapist not colluding with them. The description of these procedures will include the manifestations of unconscious (repressed or simply unreflected upon) mental processes, such processes only being of importance in so far as they shape experience and are expressed in acts, omissions or fantasies. Therapeutic change is seen to follow the patient's new insights into current patterns, the new experience entered into, especially the therapeutic relationship, and the new behaviours generated by these understandings which, in turn, break old and initiate new patterns of experience, understanding and action.

Further information requested

I see the first meeting with a patient as having two main functions: on the one hand, it is an opportunity to begin to get to know the patient and to gather information on which to base a diagnosis and treatment plan; on the other, it is an opportunity to let the patient test one's wares, by offering him or her preliminary comments or explanations of how one understands the problem, and by describing the form of therapy offered. In the case of Charlie, I felt that her first interview had provided a rich account, with no obvious omissions, and I felt confident that therapy would be possible and helpful. The main further information I sought was her response to my first thoughts and to the description of the proposed therapy (CAT). This is what I said:

> Thank you for telling me your story so well; before we finish I would like to say what I make of it so far, and suggest some things for you to do and think about before our next meeting. And I will explain how we will work together in this time-limited [sixteen sessions] therapy.
> The main themes I pick up from your story are loss, rejection and survival. The losses include your unremembered father, your mother (for the year after your father's death) and then the loss of the couple with whom you spent that year, and later the loss of your grand old grandfather, who seems to have been the one most able to show you love and value, and whom you keep alive in you through the work you have chosen to do.
> The rejections are many; you would have been aborted had it been possible, you should have been a boy, you were wrong for being ill and wrong for being well, your intelligence was not acknowledged, you were 'only' a council estate

girl at secondary school. I think the result of all this was at one level, a quiet determination to make your own life, but attached to that you acquired a (totally irrational) guilt for being. You have been made to feel that your life and success have been won at the cost of others, most recently in connection with your sister's polycystic kidneys, while the only way to your mother's care seemed to be through your own illness.

Your strengths are obvious to all but yourself, I suspect; despite the losses and rejections you have made a good career, a good marriage and have been a good parent. What brings you to therapy now (and you are uncertain if you 'deserve' it) is the echoing voice of your mother – in your head and in reality – a voice which locks you into a battle between compliance and defiance but which does not leave you free to choose outside that pair of opposites.

In therapy you will have the chance to remember the past and review the present; we cannot change what happened but we can look at the conclusions which you drew from it and the strategies you evolved to deal with it, some of which may no longer be appropriate today. To help you start on that task, I would like you to take away the 'Psychotherapy File' (see below). This contains instructions in self-monitoring, and I would like you to follow these by noting the main occasions each day on which you find yourself in your thoughts commenting on your actions in a way which comes from your mother. Note both what triggers these comments and what they consist of. The rest of the file describes a range of ways in which people may continue to operate in ways which are restricting but hard to revise; the last section on 'snags', for example, applies I think to you. But read it through and mark any that you think are true of you and we will discuss these next time.

One other task might help, but you may prefer to leave it until later. This would be to write a letter to your mother; not a letter to be sent but a letter to spell out what you wish to say and wish she could hear. But, as I say, that can wait.

We will meet each week and after one or two more meetings and your 'homework' I will write a fuller account of how I see the problems, as they were and as they now affect you. We will go through this together so you can change or add bits; the revised letter and a list of the main problems, and of the main ways in which you may still undermine yourself, will be the agenda for the remaining sessions.

I expect that in some ways you will think that it is too much, in other ways it will never by enough . . . But I think that you will be able to work well and get something of value from it. Do you have any questions about that plan, or does it feel OK?

Charlie (predictably) was happy to cooperate with this plan. As it was not possible to meet for two weeks on this occasion, we arranged for the completed file and the self-monitoring diary to be posted to me before the next 'meeting'.

The psychotherapy file

An aid to understanding ourselves better

We have all had just one life and what has happened to us, and the sense we made of this, colours the way we see ourselves and others. How we see things for us, how things are, and how we go about our lives seems 'obvious and right'. Sometimes, however, our familiar ways of understanding and acting can be the source of our problems. In order to solve our difficulties, we may need to learn to recognize how what we do makes things worse. We can then work out new ways of thinking and acting.

These pages are intended to suggest ways of thinking about what you do; recognizing your particular patterns is the first step in learning to gain more control and happiness in your life.

Keeping a diary of your moods and behaviour

Symptoms, bad moods, unwanted thoughts or behaviours that come and go can be better understood and controlled if you learn to notice when they happen and what starts them off.

If you have a particular symptom or problem of this sort, start keeping a diary. The diary should be focused on a particular mood, symptom or behaviour, and should be kept every day if possible. Try to record this sequence:

1 How you were feeling about yourself and others and the world before the problem came on.
2 Any external event, or any thought or image in your mind that was going on when the trouble started, or what seemed to start it off.

3 Once the trouble started, what were the thoughts, images or feelings you experienced.

By noticing and writing down in this way what you do and think at these times, you will learn to recognize and eventually have more control over how you act and think at the time. It is often the case that bad feelings like resentment, depression or physical symptoms are the result of ways of thinking and acting that are unhelpful. Diary keeping in this way gives you the chance to learn better ways of dealing with things.

It is helpful to keep a daily record for 1–2 weeks, then to discuss what you have recorded with your therapist or counsellor.

PATTERNS THAT DO NOT WORK, BUT ARE HARD TO BREAK

There are certain ways of thinking and acting that do not achieve what we want, but which are hard to change. Read through the lists on the following pages and mark how far you think they apply to you.

Applies strongly ++ Applies + Does not apply 0

1 TRAPS

Traps are things we cannot escape from. Certain kinds of thinking and acting result in a 'vicious circle' when, however hard we try, things seem to get worse instead of better. Trying to deal with feeling bad about ourselves, we think and act in ways that tend to confirm our badness.

Examples of Traps

1 *Fear of Hurting Others Trap*

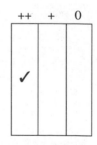

Feeling fearful of hurting others* we keep our feelings inside, or put our own needs aside. This tends to allow other people to ignore or abuse us in various ways, which then leads to our feeling, or being, childishly angry. When we see ourselves behaving like this, it confirms our belief that we shouldn't be aggressive and reinforces our avoidance of standing up for our rights.

* *People often get trapped in this way because they mix up aggression and assertion. Mostly, being assertive – asking for our rights – is perfectly acceptable. People who do not respect our rights as human beings must either be stood up to or avoided.*

2 *Depressed Thinking Trap*

Feeling depressed, we are sure we will manage a task or social situation badly. Being depressed, we are probably not as effective as we can be, and the depression leads us to exaggerate how badly we handled things. This makes us feel more depressed about ourselves.

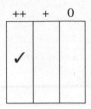

3 *Trying to Please Trap*

Feeling uncertain about ourselves and anxious not to upset others, we try to please people by doing what they seem to want. As a result (1) we end up being taken advantage of by others which makes us angry, depressed or guilty, from which our uncertainty about ourselves is confirmed; or (2) sometimes we feel out of control because of the need to please, and start hiding away, putting things off, letting people down, which makes other people angry with us and increases our uncertainty.

4 *Avoidance Trap*

We feel ineffective and anxious about certain situations, such as crowded streets, open spaces, social gatherings. We try to go back into these situations, but feel even more anxiety. Avoiding them makes us feel better, so we stop trying. However, by constantly avoiding situations, our lives are limited and we come to feel increasingly ineffective and anxious.

5 *Social Isolation Trap*

Feeling under-confident about ourselves and anxious not to upset others, we worry that others will find us boring or stupid, so we don't look at people or respond to friendliness. People then see us as unfriendly, so we become more isolated from which we are convinced we are boring and stupid – and become more under-confident.

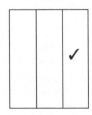

6 *Low Self-esteem Trap*

Feeling worthless we feel that we cannot get what we want because (a) we will be punished, (b) that others will reject or abandon us, or (c) as if anything good we get is bound to go away or turn sour. Sometimes it feels as if we must punish ourselves for being weak. From this we feel that everything is hopeless, so we give up trying to do anything which confirms and increases our sense of worthlessness.

2 DILEMMAS (False choices and narrow options)

We often act as we do, even when we are not completely happy with it, because the only other ways we can imagine, seem as bad or even worse. Sometimes we assume connections that are not necessarily the case – as in 'if I do "x" then "y" will follow'. These false choices can be described as either/or or if/then dilemmas. We often don't realize that we see things like this, but we act as if these were the only possible choices.

Do you act as if any of the following false choices rule your life? Recognizing them is the first step to changing them.

Choices about myself: I act AS IF:

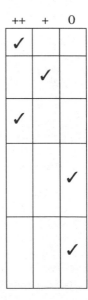

1 Either I keep feelings bottled up or I risk being rejected, hurting others, or making a mess.
2 Either I feel I spoil myself and am greedy or I deny myself things and punish myself and feel miserable.
3 If I try to be perfect, I feel depressed and angry; If I don't try to be perfect, I feel guilty, angry and dissatisfied.
4 If I must, then I won't; it is as if when faced with a task I must either gloomily submit or passively resist (other people's wishes, or even my own feel too demanding, so I put things off, avoid them).
5 If I must not then I will; it is as if the only proof of my existence is my resistance (other people's rules, or even my own feel too restricting, so I break rules and do things which are harmful to me).

6 If other people aren't expecting me to do things, look after them, etc., then I feel anxious, lonely and out of control. | | | ✓ |
7 If I get what I want, I feel childish and guilty; if I don't get what I want, I feel frustrated, angry and depressed. | ✓ | | |
8 Either I keep things (feelings, plans) in perfect order, or I fear a terrible mess. | | | ✓ |

Choices about how we relate to others: I behave with others AS IF:

	++	+	0
1 Either I'm involved with someone and likely to get hurt or I don't get involved and stay in charge, but remain lonely.			✓
2 Either I stick up for myself and nobody likes me, or I give in and get put on by others and feel cross and hurt.			✓
3 Either I'm a brute or a martyr (secretly blaming the other).		✓	
4 (a) With others either I'm safely wrapped up in bliss or in combat;			✓
(b) If in combat, then I'm either a bully or a victim.			✓
5 Either I look down on other people, or I feel they look down on me.		✓	
6 (a) Either I'm sustained by the admiration of others whom I admire or I feel exposed;		✓	
(b) If exposed, then I feel either contemptuous of others or I feel contemptible.		✓	
7 Either I'm involved with others and feel engulfed, taken over or smothered, or I stay safe and uninvolved but feel lonely and isolated.			✓
8 When I'm involved with someone whom I care about, then either I have to give in or they have to give in.			✓
9 When I'm involved with someone whom I depend on, then either I have to give in or they have to give in.		✓	
10 As a woman, either I have to do what others want or I stand up for my rights and get rejected.		✓	
11 As a man, either I can't have any feelings or I am an emotional mess.			

3 SNAGS

Snags are what is happening when we say, 'I want to have a better life, or I want to change my behaviour but . . .'. Sometimes this comes from how we or our families thought about us when we were young, such as 'she was always the good child', or 'in our family we never . . .'. Sometimes the snags come from the important people in our lives not wanting us to change, or not able to cope with what our changing means to them. Often the resistance is more indirect, as when a parent, husband or wife becomes ill or depressed when we begin to get better.

In other cases, we seem to 'arrange' to avoid pleasure or success, or if they come, we have to pay in some way, by depression, or by spoiling things. Often this is because, as children, we came to feel guilty if things went well for us, or felt that we were envied for good luck or success. Sometimes we have come to feel responsible, unreasonably, for things that went wrong in the family, although we may not be aware that this is so. It is helpful to learn to recognize how this sort of pattern is stopping you getting on with your life, for only then can you learn to accept your right to a better life and begin to claim it.

You may get quite depressed when you begin to realize how often you stop your life being happier and more fulfilled. It is important to remember that it's not being stupid or bad, but rather that:

(a) We do these things because this is the way we learned to manage best when we were younger.

(b) We don't have to keep on doing them now we are learning to recognize them.

(c) By changing our behaviour, we can learn to control not only our own behaviour, but we also change the way other people behave to us.

(d) Although it may seem that others resist the changes we want for ourselves (for example, our parents or our partners), we often underestimate them; if we are firm about our right to change, those who care for us will usually accept the change.

Do you recognize that you feel limited in your life:

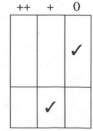

	++	+	0
1 For fear of the response of others, e.g. I must sabotage success for example as if it deprives others, as if others may envy me or as if there are not enough good things to go around.			✓
2 By something inside yourself, e.g. I must sabotage good things as if I don't deserve them.		✓	

4 DIFFICULT AND UNSTABLE STATES OF MIND

Some people find it difficult to keep control over their behaviour and experience because things feel very difficult and different at times. Indicate which, if any of the following, apply to you:

	++	+	0
1 How I feel about myself and others can be unstable; I can switch from one state of mind to a completely different one.			✓
2 Some states may be accompanied by intense, extreme and uncontrollable emotions.		✓	
3 Others by emotional blankness, feeling unreal, or feeling muddled.		✓	
4 Some states are accompanied by feeling intensely guilty or angry with myself, wanting to hurt myself.	✓		
5 Or by feeling that others can't be trusted, are going to let me down, or hurt me.		✓	
6 Or by being unreasonably angry or hurtful to others.		✓	
7 Sometimes the only way to cope with some confusing feelings is to blank them off and feel emotionally distant from others.		✓	

The diary

Charlie kept the diary for twelve days, reporting a range of episodes from both home and work. The first episode she reported was going to a workshop on massage techniques; on discovering that all the other participants had some NHS experience, and when asked why she was there, she was 'overwhelmed with inadequacy' and felt about '2 cm high'. This offers an example of the low self-esteem trap identified in the file. Examples of irrational guilt included her response to the fact that her husband 'phoned their son after an exam (she should have thought of that) and the fact that she was upset and depressed by the news of a friend's puerperal psychosis: a reaction which was 'wrong' in this context.

A number of episodes were recorded in which the argument with her 'mother in her head' was successfully pursued: she bought clothes for her daughter's taste, whereas her mother had always chosen hers for her; she 'spoils' her by arranging music lessons (but friends say she pushes her children too hard in out-of-school activities); she spends a bank holiday gardening and reading: 'this is NOT the right thing to do at any time and makes me feels very guilty. It doesn't stop me doing it though'. She explains 'my mother always used to complain about me "getting your head stuck into a book" when there was work to be done, so . . . it became my greatest pleasure'. This links with an account of the accumulating chaos in the living room, the proposed tidying finally being accomplished jointly with her husband, though earlier, when he picked up books from the floor, she recorded: 'I think – or rather my mother would have said – I should have done that'.

It will be evident that this way of therapy involves a lot of work from both patient and therapist. Much of this could be described as 'cognitive', involving thinking, self-observation and writing. The use of writing generates, I believe, more careful thinking and provides a source which can be referred to and reflected upon in between the sessions. The aim of this rapid initiation is two-fold: on the one hand, to create, right from the start, a general high level 'theory' about a patient's difficulties, to which the past and current issues can be referred; on the other, to initiate a relationship in which both patient and therapist are actively engaged in joint work. Within the framework so formed and the safety it offers, the relationship will, as therapy proceeds, become the arena in which the patient's damaging procedures are not only described, but also enacted. The therapist's recognition and acceptance of these will be accompanied by a consistent refusal to reciprocate in the expected ways; in this way, the cognitive aspects set the stage for analytic work.

Assessment

On the basis of the first meetings and the paperwork done by Charlie, I feel that assessment is largely completed and that therapy has already begun. There are still some questions I will need to ask with the aim of excluding conditions which might call for alternative treatments, and if those are not covered in the course of the next session or two, I will remind myself to bring them up. I do not feel that she gives evidence of a severe level of depression which might need medication, but the routine questions about sleep, energy and concentration should be asked. Some symptoms are not always volunteered, such as eating disorders or obsessional problems, and direct questions about these are appropriate. The family history of psychological disorders and her personal medical history and state of health should also be enquired after if I have not got the answers in the course of our undirected conversation. I prefer to leave these questions in this way rather than to start with a formal psychiatric history-taking, which risks setting the pattern of sessions along traditional doctor–patient lines.

In the case of Charlie, I do not expect to find out much more than I already know through such enquiries; I see her as a person who can be depressed and guilty rather easily, who has some negative beliefs about herself which prevent her fully enjoying her life. She is also someone who has personal strengths, capacities and achievements; and who, despite a rather barren childhood, has a capacity for good relationships. Moreover, she has already been actively self-reflective in trying to understand why she can still be dominated by the judgements derived from her mother, which she rejects. In the sphere of action she can often overcome this negative voice, but she pays with irrational guilt and depression. The balance of strengths and capacities suggest that there is every reason to believe that therapy will be helpful. Her responses to the first homework assignment were positive; while this could be seen as placatory, and may to an extent be so, the products were helpful, and this piece of work has established that the style of this therapy is cooperative and that we will both work at it.

The picture of Charlie's personality which I have formed is of someone for whom others are seen as actually or potentially critical, conditional or rejecting. These attitudes also determine her relation to herself. Her response varies from striving to please and compliance on the one hand to guilty rebellion on the other. Through the filter of these assumptions she can sometimes and in some ways experience pleasure in assertion and a feeling of being accepted, but these feelings are often attacked or paid for as if she were not entitled to them. Her coming to therapy is a step along the road to self-acceptance and to challenging these negative patterns.

In terms of the emerging transference/counter-transference patterns of my relationship with Charlie, my first response is one of liking this person and respecting her struggle. I would like to see her rebellious energy channelled into autonomy and assertiveness. I note that I have not yet seen evidence of her *enacting* the critical, conditional and rejecting role, but suspect that it may be lurking in the wings. There is a risk that she will compliantly accept therapy within her unusual terms, and a danger that any real gains may be dismantled by her guilty self-sabotage. Childhood figures who provided much needed care are, I often feel, the therapist's ancestors; they have prepared a place within the person which we may occupy. In Charlie's case, I am aware of my identification with her grandfather (whose political attitudes are close to mine), and while this may well be a positive factor it will be important to guard against idealization.

My main feeling, however, is that a good working partnership can be established between her self-observing self and me, in which she will learn to develop and apply the tools of CAT. If all goes well, she will take away from therapy an internalized person and internalized ways of thinking and feeling about herself which will enable her to claim her life more fully.

At our next meeting, on the basis of the psychotherapy file, the diary and our one hour 'meeting', I produced my draft reformulation which Michael read to Charlie:

> Thank you for checking the psychotherapy file and for completing the diary, which I found very useful. I think I am ready today to give you the provisional written account of how I understand your story and what I see the focus of therapy to be. Let me just read it out and then we will go through it to make sure it sounds right to you, and to change it if necessary.
>
> Your early life was marked by a series of painful losses and rejections, and from your mother you learned to feel bad for being a failed abortion, for not being a boy, for being or not being ill, and so on. In your adult life these themes have recurred: your terminated pregnancy and your sister's recent illness were echoes, but more importantly, despite at one level being perfectly aware of your own competence and right to a life, you are dogged by irrational guilt and by a continual battle. It is as if each choice is about complying with or defying your mother (or 'mother in your head').
>
> Your completion of the psychotherapy file identifies many of the ways in which you are still controlled by the lessons of childhood. Thus your fear of hurting others, your depressed thinking, your trying to please, your need to avoid situations, your social isolation trap and your low self-esteem are all manifestations of a rejection of or a lack of trust in yourself. Why do these persist when you know that as a wife, mother and worker you are loved and respected by others?
>
> Part of the reason is the way that the Traps are hard to get out of; the beliefs lead to ways of acting that produce consequences which seem to reinforce the beliefs. Then take a look at the Dilemmas about yourself which you ticked: the false choices between *either* keeping feelings bottled up *or* making a mess, between *either* trying to be perfect and feeling angry and depressed *or* not trying and feeling guilty, and between *either* guiltily getting what you want *or* angrily

not getting it, are all, I think, reflections of the way in which so many situations seem to require you *either* to resemble and obey your mother, *or* defy her; there is no space for all that you might *choose* to do for yourself. Your diary reported examples of these, as you know. The next page, describing dilemmas in how you relate to others, has several single pluses. These suggest that the world is a rather dangerous place; people are out to get you, control you or dismiss you and the only apparent alternative is to get, control or dismiss them. I think we can guess where this model of 'them' comes from: your survival as a child was probably due to your capacity to resist and react, if only internally. But if you feel you have to go into most relationships with your guard up, you tend to extract similar stances in others. Finally, you give a single plus to the second Snag where I would be inclined to put two. I sense, from your diary, a pervasive inability to consult your own wishes, value your own judgements or live your own life without paying, for example, with guilt or depression. We will look at it together to see how far you agree with that judgement.

So . . . to sum up. You have come to therapy with an awareness that you are not free of your mother's negative influence and with a proneness to depression and irrational guilt. One measure of how therapy helps you will be in terms of these symptoms or feelings. Underlying these feelings are what I call Target Problem Procedures, by which I mean the ways in which you feel, think and act evoke responses from others in a mode which maintains your negative state. I have summarized these in three descriptions, which I have written as in your own voice:

1 I live AS IF I am a bad person, even though I know I am not. I reinforce this assumption in the ways described in the file in the Traps which I ticked (fear of hurting others, depressed thinking, trying to please, avoidance, social isolation, low self-esteem).
2 Because so much of the time I seem to believe that what I do is EITHER to obey and be like my mother OR to defy her, I reduce the options open to me to absurdly polarized dilemmas, as identified in the file. Doing this serves to reinforce my polarized way of seeing things.
3 I have a sabotaging part of me, often appearing as my mother's voice. It does not respect my needs and feelings

and this undermines my intentions and makes me pay for happiness or success with depression and guilt.

We need to go through this and will doubtless change some details and wording, after which I will make a fair copy for each of us. [My aim will be to get these 'problem procedures' spelled out as far as possible in Charlie's own words and metaphors.] The first task of therapy is to get smart at recognizing these patterns as they occur; to do this you could continue to keep a diary, recording the events of the day and then going through to identify when you have repeated one of the patterns. We will also need to watch out for them during our meetings.

As you get good at recognizing them, we can begin to consider alternative ways of proceeding. You will also probably find that half-forgotten memories and feelings related to these patterns and to their childhood origins will come more vividly to mind, sometimes painfully. But, as you learn to explore alternative ways of proceeding and develop a new, focused ability to watch what you do, so you can choose to do what you want, therapy will be giving you a new voice and companion to set beside the maternal voice in your head.

My part will be to watch out for the way you may fear to speak your mind, especially when you feel critical (as sometimes you are bound to), and to guard against the part of you which will dismantle what we do because it is what you want and need.

How does that sound?

Charlie's first comment was that 'it sounds mostly good, although I'm not sure I understand some of the things you say'. She went on to apologize that the diary had been boring, explaining that frequent references to housework were not typical, but reflected the focus upon these areas in which her mother's voice was prominent. In later written comments, she said, 'I don't understand what you mean by "that part of you which will dismantle what we do because it is what you want and need". Do you mean I deliberately set out to deny myself what I want? Having just written this, I have just remembered several recent incidents, all of them trivial, when that is precisely what I did . . . if it works that way for small, unimportant things, then it probably does even more for things that matter'.

With this comment Charlie's assessment could be said to be over; she has shown that she is able to think and work in the way which characterizes this particular form of therapy.

Therapeutic possibilities

One can seldom be certain about the outcome of therapy. Research suggests that the outcome tends to be worse in patients with more severe disturbances, in those with poorly integrated personality structures and, in particular, among those with major problems in maintaining relationships. Those who can recall no good figures from their early life are likely to be deficient in self-acceptance and untrusting of others, including the therapist. Certain symptoms, such as severe obsessional or major eating disorders, are also resistant to help. None of these factors are an absolute bar to therapy, but the fact that all are absent in the case of Charlie makes the outlook for a good outcome pretty rosy.

It is probable that Charlie could benefit from a variety of therapeutic approaches; the therapist's acceptance, the improved morale and the provision of a new way of thinking about herself common to most therapies, would combine with her own capacities to produce change. But these factors alone are not always enough, both because those living in relation to the patient frequently resist their changing, and because therapy itself may be undermined by the very process it seeks to modify.

In CAT, these issues are addressed from the beginning. The explicit way of working and the early involvement of the patient in joint work recruit the patient's capacities and limit the extent to which the therapist may be unrealistically depended upon or attacked. Resistance, unless in response to unhelpful therapeutic methods, is understood to be no more than the inevitable mobilization in the therapy relationship of those issues for which help is sought, and offers an opportunity to demonstrate to the patient how these procedures present. It is often helpful to anticipate this, as in the reformulation letter above, so that their arrival can be greeted in a matter-of-fact, non-judgemental way.

To be able to work in this way, patients need not be sophisticated or 'psychologically minded' when first seen. In Charlie's case, we have a fluent, intelligent and self-reflective person, who has already shown a capacity to think about herself in new ways. The only obstacle to successful therapy in her case could be her too ready acceptance of her limits and her guilty sense of not deserving help. Her own fear was expressed as follows: 'I think my main problem may well be that I have behaved in this way for so long that I can no longer sort out what I want from what I think others want of me'. This fear is not backed up by our research in CAT, which shows no relation between outcome and length of history, but her comment is a warning. The time-limited nature of CAT and the emphasis on early, crisp descriptions and ways of working could be all too persuasive. It will be essential to guard against 'curing' Charlie in ways which are within the terms of her problems; in particular, once she has grasped and recognized what she has been doing to restrict herself, she should be left to work out what to do instead, in her own terms and at her own pace. Much of this will take place after the therapy is over.

The course of therapy

Every therapy is unique and the only certain predictions I can make about the likely course of Charlie's therapy are about those areas which I can determine. Essentially, these concern the arrangement of therapy as regards times and places and the fact that this is a time-limited, sixteen-session therapy. This will be explicitly contracted, and it will be made clear that missed sessions, unless notified in advance, will not be replaced. Within this time-frame, we will determine our particular way of working together.

Charlie had talked freely and expressed feelings openly in her first session, launching into an autobiographical account and linking this with her present difficulties without prompting. This suggested that she had pre-existing ideas about therapy and that she was basically capable of trust: but, especially in her manner, there was some pressure of anxiety (but perhaps no more than the situation warranted). The fullness of the account she gave and her own gloss upon it made reformulation an easy task in this case: in writing my draft my main aim was to show how, although she clearly knew what her significant experiences had been, she was still operating in the present with restrictive procedures derived from them.

Therapy has a beginning, a middle and an end; in the case of CAT, reformulation represents the beginnings and its completion usually seals a good working relationship between the therapist and the patient. At this stage, having agreed on a description of the damaging procedures, the second stage of using these descriptions to recognize them begins. The third stage of the therapy (i.e. termination) will be on the agenda from now on, and the third stage of CAT (i.e. revision) will have begun by then, but will not be completed. Part of the work of learning recognition will involve specific tasks; for example, Charlie's realization that she did indeed deny herself what she wanted will be followed by her keeping a diary for one or two weeks in which she specifically monitors this tendency. But the setting and receiving back of such assignments will only occupy a small proportion of our time in the sessions, most of which will be left unstructured, as was the first interview. What Charlie does with this time will, of course, reflect who she is, and it is a safe prediction that the stories she brings and the way she relates to me will include many examples of the identified procedures. In this process, my own awareness of her procedures will alert me to ways in which she might, for example, seek to placate me, or fear hurting me, or might demonstrate her underlying belief that one or other of us is going to do the other down. When this occurs I will point it out, providing a living example of how she responds to these patterns and exploring alternatives with her.

In this way, my main interventions will be demonstrations rather than interpretations. The relationship of interpreter to interpreted subject is an unequal one. The claim to know another's unconscious processes and desires can only be taken on trust and may undermine an already precarious trust in one's own judgements. What is important about unconscious processes is their manifestation in acts, omissions and fantasies which can be described. For example, Charlie's 'snag', whereby she denies herself what she wants, could be interpreted as the result of unconscious guilt or as a defence against unconscious greed. What we *know* is that it happens, and what we can plausibly suspect is that it is a pattern derived from her mother's attitudes to her and her sister and from the many other factors which made her feel undeserving. Having described (or re-described) this pattern, we can question whether it is just or necessary, and having recognized it, she can begin to choose not to repeat it. The evidence for the pattern and its appearance is as available to Charlie as it is to me, and, having learned to see it, her confidence in her self-observing capacity is enhanced rather than undermined.

As a consequence of the established therapy relationship and the new understandings summarized in the reformulation, patients become less anxious and defensive. As a result, in parallel with the working on recognition and revision, there is usually a return of, or intensification of, feelings and memories from the past. In Charlie's case, it is bound to be her experience that the losses involved in her father's death, in being sent away from home and then in losing her 'substitute parents', represented an unmanageable emotional load. This may have been compounded by the way in which children are liable to take responsibility for the events around them, and this could be another source of Charlie's irrational guilt. It will very probably be the case that during this therapy deep and painful feelings from that time will emerge. This may be associated with the loss of the therapist, an event on the agenda at every meeting. Brief therapy, in its explicit acceptance that it does not and cannot make up for the past, can allow patients the experience of getting something even though it is not enough, and of experiencing a manageable loss. Through this, some of the need to avoid memory and feeling can be shed, and some of the self-blame jettisoned. On the way to recovery, a period of mourning for the waste and losses of the past is often experienced.

The degree to which we can explore these levels of feeling will depend on Charlie's capacities and the strength of our relationship. I feel optimistic on both these counts, which reflects both my therapeutic temperament and experience of CAT in many more disturbed patients, and my evaluation of what we have done so far. The worst outcome for brief therapy is that a need for further therapy has been established, but I will be surprised if that is the case with Charlie.

There are, however, some areas of uncertainty which may affect the course of the therapy. These derive from her intense rejection of her mother, and her incomplete separation from her. In rejecting her mother's critical, undermining stance, that part of her which is capable of similar behaviour and feeling is hard to acknowledge and has not so far been mentioned. This is reflected in her polarizing of the ways of relating to others (as in the psychotherapy file dilemmas: 'brute or martyr', 'look down on or be looked down on', 'if exposed then either contemptuous or contemptible') and in her usual 'choice' of the inferior role. This, and her need for admiration from admired others (see the file) indicate some of the features of a narcissistic personality. Underlying the choice of the inferior role (and this is a hypothesis I would suggest to Charlie, not an authoritative interpretation), I suspect that early childhood rivalries – with her mother for her father and with her sister for her mother – may have played a part. Part of therapy may be a seeking of a way in which these destructive feelings, derived from modelling on her mother and from early envy and jealousy, may be acknowledged and controlled rather than denied.

If these issues do not emerge in the therapy relationship and if Charlie can see that they might be explored, some more active, experimental techniques might be useful. The letter to her mother, suggested at our first meeting, might be one way; it is often surprising how difficult it is to write down negative feelings even in a letter that will never be posted. Alternatively, an 'empty chair' conversation with her mother could be explored, or more general explorations of feeling through writing or painting might be proposed.

Related to these issues are questions of what it means to be a woman. In the first interview she remarked that she had not thought about what her childhood meant in respect of 'me and men'. It appears that she has married a loving and generous man, but it is worth noting that she gives a single plus to the psychotherapy file dilemma, 'As a woman either I have to do what others want or I stand up for my rights and get rejected'; and that, as a graduate she is under-employed. These are areas which I will certainly wish to explore further.

As the end of therapy approaches, both I and Charlie will have to face what has and has not been achieved. For my part, although experience tells me that the main effect of working within a time limit is to deepen and quicken change, I will be aware of opportunities missed, of unmet needs and of regret. For Charlie, as I suggested above, it may well be that ending will echo her childhood losses and will evoke both sadness and anger. These feelings, especially the latter, may be concealed or only hinted at, and it will be important to make it clear that they are recognized and acceptable. At the penultimate session, I will present Charlie with a 'goodbye letter' and will, I hope, receive one from her. My letter will rehearse the problems and problem procedures listed in the reformulation and describe as concretely as possible what change has been achieved. Just as each session will have been ended with a review of how these issues are being recognized and revised (usually in the form of a rating or graph), so the whole therapy needs to be evaluated; these procedures are the way of teaching the patient accurate self-observation. There is no point, therefore, in offering bland reassurances or blanket optimism, and there is every need to describe or anticipate feelings of disappointment or more powerful negative reactions. However, what was good should also be named, and 'permission' to internalize the therapist and to take away and use the tools of therapy should be included. Unfinished business, and ways of continuing to work at the problems, should be named, and the arrangements for follow-up (usually two to three months later) should be recorded. The patient's letter naturally has no prescribed form, but he or she is encouraged to be as accurate and frank as possible. Both letters are usually read out, and the therapist's, after any corrections have been made through discussion, is given to the patient.

This letter and the earlier reformulation, and any other written or diagrammatic 'tools', represent 'transitional objects', created in the space between patient and therapist and, in time, being taken in and becoming part of the self. I believe the use of concrete written tools makes termination more manageable and is a way of guarding against the patient's forgetting or devaluation of therapy when facing the pains of terminating therapy.

Problem areas

Many of the problems in this (in general, not very problematic) patient have been considered above. There should not be any difficulty in maintaining an effective working relationship with Charlie, and the fact that her problem procedures are likely to be enacted with me means that we can recognize and revise them 'in the room'. Linking with this her monitoring of them in daily life should offer a dense experience of re-evaluating herself. However, despite the evidence of her strength and the basic goodness of her close relationships, she may find it hard to let go of her habitual procedures, especially those which keep her away from destructive feelings.

Her acceptance of brief therapy (usually, if incorrectly, understood to imply an incomplete or superficial one) may well reflect that she feels that she does not deserve help. It could also be taken as a reason for not getting involved. The pattern of high activity required in the early sessions might reinforce compliance or might generate the equally unhelpful pattern of passive resistance that characterizes her relationship to housework. Too great an emphasis on the tasks and concepts could yield some gains, for example in modifying her traps through graded behavioural change. But it would, I suspect, leave unmodified her way of polarizing options and her self-denials and undoings. On the other hand, an exclusively psychodynamic approach might fail to recruit her to therapy, being frustrating to someone who coped from an early age with no support until her marriage, and who, if she stayed in therapy, might become more of a brute than a martyr in that relationship. As CAT combines elements from both approaches, the technical challenge will be to get the balance right, recruiting her abilities and providing ideas and a relationship for her to use, but ready for the ways in which she will inadvertently damage the process. My guess is that Charlie will make a lot of progress in the early sessions, but that this will evoke her 'snag': faced with improvement she will undo it in some way. I am also concerned that her relatively satisfactory level of functioning in most areas of her life will make her doubt whether facing the distress of her childhood is really worth it. Only she can decide whether or not to go through the fire; as a therapist I would try to convince her that the gain of doing so is worth it, but she has the right to decide.

I do not think that these difficulties are related to the particular form of this therapy; any approach that is more than cosmetic would bring them to light. But there are features of CAT which, as therapy proceeds, might not be what the patient wants, even though the attempt was made to explain in advance. The ratio of demand to support is high and not everyone welcomes this; therapy is hard work and the chance of emotional pain and the rapid pace of CAT means that a lot of resilience is called for. The final judgement may depend on what is known about other therapies that friends may have been involved in: comparing her experience with the long-term dependency of psychodynamic therapy, the CAT patient may long for the support or be delighted to have escaped; or compared with a friend who has received focused cognitive-behavioural therapy, the CAT patient may envy the way in which feelings were left relatively unstirred, or be grateful to have been through experiences which were unexpected and relieving, even if painful. In the end, the proof of the pudding is in the eating; if pain and work are the prelude to greater freedom to choose and a stronger sense of self, then patients can forgive their therapists, even for being imperfect. I expect to be imperfect. I expect Charlie to have to work and to experience some pain, but on balance I expect us to overcome the problems in ways that make it worthwhile.

Criteria for successful outcome

In a therapy which aims to generate a greater capacity for accurate self-reflection, the assessment of change is an integral part of the process. In Charlie's ratings of recognition and change, made at the end of each session, and in the goodbye letter exchanged at the end of therapy, I will seek to forestall or correct any tendency to exaggerate improvement in order to please me and avoid negative feelings.

All therapy-induced change goes through a series of stages, not all of which will be achieved in every therapy. The first stage is the patient's recognition that problems exist which they are, in part at least, responsible for. The second stage is for them to understand in the most useful way possible how they do this and what therapy must aim to change. In CAT these stages are normally completed through the process of reformulation, which transforms the patient from a sufferer to an active problem-solver. I am confident that Charlie is well on the way to completing these changes.

The third stage is seldom straightforward; acceptance that one is actively maintaining one's problems and recognition of how one is doing this does not immediately free one from the tendency to continue to repeat the old patterns. Most people hope that they can change without having to change. Change may encounter internal resistance (Charlie's 'snag'), and is also likely to provoke resistance from those whose own needs are satisfied by reciprocating her old, damaging patterns. This is seldom an absolute barrier and in Charlie's case there are, at present, no obvious signs of difficulty of this sort; but as change occurs, some such signs may well be uncovered. In this area the therapeutic relationship can be crucial; my job will be both to name Charlie's invitations to collude and to manage not to do so. Awareness of my own temptations and weaknesses is essential here; I could, for example, be drawn into agreeing that we have no negative feelings to deal with in our relationship. The successful negotiation of this stage will be manifest in real changes in Charlie's behaviour and in her ability to re-negotiate those relationships in which the other resists or punishes her new procedures.

The fourth stage is one in which real intrapsychic change occurs; the punitive patterns that determine relationships with self and others are modified. In Charlie's case, these were formed in early and difficult experiences with all those on whom she most depended. The conclusions which she, as a child, drew from these experiences were registered in the form of her assumptions about what patterns were necessary, and were sustained by her continuing to operate in terms of them. Therapy offers a relationship designed to challenge the restrictive and damaging patterns. The most secure change is achieved when the therapist, and the lessons learned from him or her, is internalized as an alternative 'voice' to the hurtful ones derived from the past. The intrapsychic structures determining relationships with self and others were first formed in an interpersonal field and their revision takes place in the same way. Alongside the old negative patterns, the relationship with the respecting, honest and caring figure of the therapist can contain and override what has, up to now, dominated behaviour. This 'internal therapist' will, in due course, become an automatic part of the self. One sign that this was happening in Charlie might be her ability to cope with her mother in less stereotypic and powerless ways; as the 'internal mother' is modified and controlled by the 'internal therapist', the mother in the world may become far more manageable and even likable.

How far therapy has gone, in terms of these stages, cannot be evaluated by the patient or the therapist until the follow-up. During the process of change, anxiety, confusion, unfamiliar emotion and so on may make the patient feel worse, and at termination the mixture of pain and denial is hard to disentangle. It is the active mourning of the therapy after termination that allows internalization and the consolidation of change. In Charlie's case, I feel confident that some stable improvement will be achieved in the third stage, but there are too many unknown factors for the extent of this, and of the fourth stage to be predicted.

Further reading

Ryle, A. (1990). *Cognitive Analytic Therapy: Active Participation in Change.* Chichester: John Wiley.

Ryle, A. (ed.) (1995). *Cognitive Analytic Therapy: Developments in Theory and Practice.* Chichester: John Wiley.

CLAIRE WINTRAM

9 FEMINIST GROUP THERAPY

The therapist

I have a degree in modern languages, a teaching qualification and an MA in social work. I have followed courses in counselling survivors of rape and sexual assault run by members of a Rape Crisis Line. I have also completed courses in bereavement counselling and in counselling people who have been adopted and who want to trace their birth parent or parents.

I was a social worker and social work manager for thirteen years and taught on the MA/CQSW course at Leicester University School of Social Work for three years. Currently, I act as a supervisor for the Leicester Counselling Centre.

I became involved in groupwork with women in 1979 and this involvement has continued in both teaching and practice. As a social worker, I established and facilitated groups for women going through divorce, and for women isolated within their own community. These groups were born out of my frustration with conventional social work approaches stressing individual pathology.

I work with women survivors of all forms of violence, which is often compounded by institutional indifference. In most of the work I engage in with women (even courses on women and health or women returning to paid work), what comes to the fore are issues of oppression, and particularly the constraining fear generated by violence.

Much of my work involves trying to remove the labels of mad and/or bad that have been stuck on women over the years, and encouraging women to recognize, name and value their own strengths. I am much influenced by feminist arguments stressing the ways in which women's behaviour is interpreted as problematic and seen as a mental health issue, when in reality there are many factors of structural disadvantage contributing to events.

I work as an independent trainer and groupworker. Among many areas, I cover counselling skills, creative counselling, women and health, women and assertiveness, women and ageing, women and group-work. I use dream interpretation to understand ourselves and our lives more clearly.

My feminist beliefs have evolved over years of working with women in groups and as individuals. I believe strongly that whatever responsibility we carry for our own behaviour, it is also vital that structural factors are taken into account. I believe that it is essential to have an understanding of disadvantage and the impact it has on different women's lives and the varying strategies they find for dealing with it. I have learnt to soften the demarcation lines between teaching and therapy, where to engage in self-disclosure, and where to use my own experience as part of the teaching and therapeutic process.

I owe a debt to the staff of the Women's Therapy Centre in London, for their wonderful book, *In Our Own Hands: A Book of Self-Help Therapy*, (edited by Sheila Ernst and Lucy Goodison, Women's Press, 1992). This book is an endless source of inspirational material. I am also indebted to all the women from many different backgrounds with whom I have worked over the years, for their courage and determination in sharing their triumphs and disappointments.

My work with women concentrates on acknowledging their pain, and giving them space to express it through whichever means is most appropriate. I use relaxation and guided fantasy to enable women to regain a sense of self and wholeness. I encourage women to recognize where they can take responsibility for change and control in their lives, where what has gone wrong is not their fault. I encourage women to celebrate their creativity, resistance and resilience.

Further information requested

Charlie has a very vivid way of describing things and remembers her feelings as clearly as the events themselves. This makes it relatively easy to draw up areas of further work. I put a series of questions to Charlie:

1 *When you say that you were ill a lot throughout your childhood, was this because you were susceptible to childhood diseases (chicken pox, scarlet fever, mumps, etc.), or was it that you had a recurring illness of a different nature?*

2 *You say that somehow you were made to feel that you'd caused your father's increasing weakness as you got stronger. What were the messages you got about this? Was there ever anything explicit or was it suggested to you in any other way you can remember?*
3 *When you say that your mother suggested to you that your childhood illnesses were hypochondria, how did this happen?*

Charlie described the extreme lengths she had to go to in her childhood, to convince people of several things. Her physical health troubled her for some time. The way in which she was made to feel a burden because of this has had a lasting effect on her self-esteem. I am impressed by her determination as a child in convincing adults of her truthfulness and in her conviction that she was right about her health. These are clear examples of her strength of character, which has survived her many experiences of rejection. This determination is evident in her adult life too, and I feel it can be seen as an innate characteristic of her own and not solely as defiance of her mother.

She seems able now to identify very well with the feelings of powerlessness and outrage a child experiences. I am sure that this makes her a very good parent. This empathy is apparent in the way she describes other people's frustrations with her own behaviour. It is clear, too, that this empathy kindles her compassion and understanding for her mother. She talked about her with less criticism in answer to my questions. It is vital not to diminish the detrimental effect of Charlie's mother's behaviour on her, nor to deny the lasting impact of this. But what *is* important is that Charlie begins to see her mother as more of a fallible human being and less of a tyrant in the answers to these questions. This is significant because it is only when we accept all aspects of *ourselves* as part of us, that we can begin to understand the causes of behaviour in others, that we might repudiate. I see this as an important step in healing for Charlie. If she is able to stop expecting perfection from herself, and to stop expecting drastic and world-shattering events when she takes a particular course of action, then it is more likely that she will begin to see and accept that everyone is made up of all manner of characteristics. These may not all be desirable, but it is important to recognize what we can and cannot change. At the end of the day, we may have to choose between compromise and maintaining some relationship, or making categorical decisions that change everything.

4 *What makes you say that you must have done something for your mother only to be able to relate to you when you need her care, when you are ill?*

5 *When your mother didn't take your library books back until the last minute, were you ever able to discuss this with her, and show her how distressed it made you feel?*
6 *What was your mother's reaction when it was finally established that you had passed the eleven-plus? Can you remember?*

It is significant that Charlie felt that the only time her mother can care for her is when she is ill. There is a stark contradiction between being told that as a child she was a burden and being made to understand that she was responsible for her father's death, and then being cared for as an adult. Is her mother trying to compensate for some of the times she was unpleasant and uncaring to Charlie as a little girl? Is it the only way she can show her feelings? Is she envious, or even frightened of how she sees Charlie? A woman with a successful marriage, successful job, happy children, good health, friends – all the things her mother never had? Her mother probably *had* to try to keep control of what was happening to her as a young woman. We do not know what support *she* got from her parents, whether she was made to feel ashamed of having become pregnant outside marriage.

I am impressed, too, with Charlie's statements about loving children, that you do so because they are there. This is a feeling that she never had from her own mother. This shows the depth of her tolerance and understanding. I am sure it would be possible to work on these so that she could begin to apply them to herself. Her self-criticism seems harsh and I feel she needs to learn to be kind to herself and to respect all aspects of herself.

I find very revealing Charlie's description of her growing awareness of being able to work out what other people are thinking. Her description of herself as the child who sat in the corner watching, no doubt has contributed to her ability to observe and recall events with such clarity today. On the issue of the eleven-plus, she saw her mother as proud of her because it meant she could talk about the achievement in public, but not for the achievement in itself. This must have been an overwhelming disappointment to Charlie – not to be appreciated for what she had done all by herself.

7 *Apart from the things you say your mother told you about 'women's lot' (e.g. menstruation, putting up with sex), can you remember any other images or messages about women that you absorbed as a girl or young woman?*
8 *Can you remember what you felt about that present on your fifteenth birthday?*

9 *What did you feel about having to fulfil other people's expectations of you?*
It is important that Charlie recognizes that she *did* get positive images of women from her childhood, even if these were somewhat distorted by her mother's anger and bitterness. She has taken hold of these and used them in a very constructive way in her own life. Her determination and decisiveness in her paid job, in getting married, in having an abortion, in deciding on how to deal with her relationship with her mother, all are indications of this. She has much in her life to be proud of. I feel that her fundamental view of women is that we *do* have strength, even if it is not safe to show it all the time. I would like to know what feminism means to her, whether it is about women's independence, about changing the ways in which we live – the personal being political, about self-respect and about nurturing herself. The strength of her political commitment comes across too. However, it is important that Charlie allows herself to relax and not feel that she has to be doing something all the time. It is important to learn that 'doing nothing' is time out and restorative and necessary.

10 *After you had an abortion, can you say what it was that got in the way of you being able to talk to your husband about it?*
The information that Charlie gave about the time after her abortion, I found extremely moving. It leaves me with the feeling of a woman desperately needing comfort and someone with whom to share her distress, but who is stuck because of the responsibility *she* feels for easing her husband's pain. It is good that she was able to read material that gave her permission to see things differently and to know that grieving for her dead baby is right. I think it is wonderful that she kept, as she told me in answer to my question, the cooperation card and the identity bracelet from that time. Does she think it possible to talk about this with her husband and children? It seems as if she is hanging on to all the feelings herself. She talks about feeling unable to handle someone else's pain. I wonder whether she feels she or anyone else can handle her own. These are all issues I want to discuss with her. Sadly, I think her perception of people's difficulties in talking about death, and in particular the death of a child, are accurate. But it means that she feels she has no right to say what is on her mind. It is as though she never tried to find out whether it was possible to talk to her husband, because the risks seemed so great.

11 *When you're doing your paid job, are you aware of anything which stops your mother's voice influencing your thoughts and behaviour?*

Another area I want to work on with Charlie relates to whether her mother has or has not had experience of paid work. It is vital that Charlie has an area of life that she feels is entirely her own, but this does not mean that she cannot take pride in achievements that might display characteristics inherited from her mother. We all have aspects of our parents in us, however hard we may try to deny this. We have to take responsibility for our own actions, even when we can see inherited factors that have led us to behave in certain ways that may annoy us.

12 *When you say, 'I'm not the sort of person people like', what exactly do you mean? What sort of person do you think people like?*
As for the notion of a 'person other people like', again this was very revealing: 'People who are more ... who give back more than I do'. Is this the sort of person Charlie likes, or would like to be herself? People like all sorts of people for all sorts of different reasons, many of them inexplicable.

The answers Charlie gave to many of my questions leave me feeling that many of these areas need work on them.

Assessment

I understand Charlie to be a woman experiencing considerable conflict stemming from various sources. I see her also as a very strong woman, full of determination and courage. Her vibrancy and enthusiasm for life come across very powerfully in the transcripts. At the same time, I recognize and respect her vulnerability. I want to encourage her to see her vulnerability for what it is worth, not to suppress it and not to see it as weakness. This aspect of herself allows her to be compassionate, to empathize with others (her husband's pain, her mother's frustration and disappointment).

My perception is that Charlie recognizes – or is beginning to recognize – her own needs, but is less sure of her right to these needs, and even less sure of her right to ask for them to be met.

The structure provided by paid work, and by her responsibilities in the Governors' group, perhaps contribute to her feeling of safety and personal value in these environments. This in turn diminishes the scope there is for influences from other sources. These are areas where, as an adult woman, she functions in a way that attracts recognition and status.

It seems to me that a pattern has been built up from childhood, of feeling responsible for other people's well-being. These feelings exist at the expense of voicing and responding to her own needs. Much work with women has demonstrated this pattern, time and time again, as well as the ways in which it is reinforced by the caring responsibilities shouldered by women in most families, in different cultures. This is further reinforced, subtly and overtly through the media, religion, education, social pressure and many other ways.

Many women may need months if not years to be enabled to unearth and celebrate their spirit of creativity, whatever form this takes. With Charlie, it seems to me that she has faith and confidence in her professional and intellectual abilities and feels that people's positive response to this is valid.

In dealing with her emotional capacities and needs, I feel that Charlie has been silenced. This embargo on emotional self-expression stems from her childhood experiences of:

- feeling unloved by her mother,
- feeling unappreciated by her mother,
- being seen as a burden,
- feeling unwanted because of knowing that she might have been aborted,
- feeling responsible for the emotional and physical health of the rest of the family,
- being disbelieved and discredited at school about her ill-health and about her academic achievements.

This has left a huge gap in her self-esteem and her considerable achievements appear to have occurred *despite* rather than *because* of these experiences. I think she has been left with an acute lack of trust in her own emotional self and in most other people's positive feelings towards her. She does not consider herself loveable *as she is* because she did not have that unconditional security as a child. So now it is very hard to believe anyone who says they like her or love her simply for herself.

I imagine Charlie as an immensely likeable woman, from the spirit and sense of humour and self-awareness that come through the transcripts. I feel that she is a very warm person with considerable compassion and insight. These attributes seem to me to have been stifled and devalued because of the messages absorbed about her *mother's* desperate need to survive. Charlie appears to understand the socio-economic context within which her mother managed to bring her and her sister up. But it is almost as if her highly developed political awareness – coupled with the denial of positive feeling experienced as a child – have overridden any notion of permission to *need and feel*. The fact that she finds it almost impossible to make the first move in any relationship, whatever its nature, suggests her fear of rejection, of being found wanting. It is like a cycle of 'If I don't take risks, don't get involved, then at least it's safe and I won't get hurt'. I have a very strong feeling that Charlie does not want it to be like this, that she *does* want to engage more fully in a life of friendships and emotional commitment outside her immediate family. But it seems as though fear is a major factor in her difficulties in this sphere. The fear itself is completely understandable, because she has had so much experience of rejection in the past. However, if there is to be any movement, Charlie needs to be encouraged to see how obstructive that fear is. It is as if there is a split in her self-respect. Her mother has been demonized to some extent, and it is important that Charlie does not sustain this approach. I see it as vital that Charlie is given permission to be hurt, angry, disappointed, confused, about her mother's behaviour towards her as a child. Her awareness about and compassion towards her mother, which I feel grow throughout the transcripts, are very important in terms of not making her mother responsible for all her negative experiences. But at the same time, her awareness must not be used to erase the pain she felt and still feels. I have the impression of someone whose emotional responses are frozen because of the hurt. She said she was described as an iceberg – is that because of what is hidden or is it also because she *seems* cold? She does not *feel* cold, she feels alive and lively. I think the iceberg is a survival mechanism, a vicious circle of, 'I'll appear cold and then I'll attract no-one, and then I won't get hurt because I won't be rejected, but at the same time, I'm trapped and hurting in this icy loneliness'. As a child, that iceberg must have given her protection in times of confusion and pain – almost like suspended animation – and now the time has come for the thaw to begin.

Another major factor is the abortion Charlie had. Charlie's experience here is sadly so common. The loss of a baby, whether through abortion, termination or miscarriage, is so often seen as a routine part of women's lives, that it is not afforded the time and space it needs and deserves.

It *is* loss, it *is* bereavement. Charlie's mementoes of the baby are very poignant and very important. It is wonderful that she has kept them and that she affords the dead baby equal status with her surviving children. This is a major step in the healing process for her. She needs permission to mourn, to grieve, to be encouraged to unlearn her guilt. She needs to recognize that talking with Andrew could bring them closer, that sharing the pain might be cathartic, not more of a burden. She needs to know that she did not kill her baby, that she is keeping its spirit alive, that it is all right to have regrets, but that it is important not to let them drag her down.

My assessment of her acknowledges her confusion, her sadness, her trapped, suspended pain, but also her openness and willingness to engage with new perspectives on all of these. The detailed content of the first transcript and her willingness to give such full answers to the additional questions, and the obvious thought that went into those, reinforce this view. It seems to me that she is standing at the top of a hill; one way lies familiarity and suppressed anger and pain, the other way lies the unknown, but also the possibilities of major change.

I have the strong feeling of a woman on the brink of a lot of self-realization.

Therapeutic possibilities

There are very strong indications that feminist therapy and groupwork will be successful with Charlie. Groupwork offers support, relaxation, the opportunity to take time out through different forms of participation. It gives Charlie the chance to listen to other women's stories and to compare those with her own. It gives her the chance to receive compliments from more than one person. Bringing any group of women together and looking at self-esteem, depending on how the group is facilitated and the ground rules agreed upon, will almost inevitably lead to discussion about a range of experiences that include abortion, miscarriage, violence, self-worth. This will give Charlie, in a safe environment, the scope to think about the fact that some of what she feels is to do with the ways in which many women in western society have been brought up to see themselves, and is not an innate fault.

It is possible that Charlie may feel threatened by being part of a group; she may decide that she wants more time devoted to herself exclusively.

The indications to me that my approach to therapy might work are that Charlie seems to want to change things in her emotional life. She is aware of pain, and however difficult it is to name it, she *is* prepared to discuss experiences. I feel a strong sense of empathy with her and recognize much that I have worked with in other women. I am confident, therefore, that I could offer her some ways of increasing her self-esteem and encourage her to use her energy more productively. I want to facilitate her grieving in relation to the abortion that might help free her from some of the guilt she feels about this. Although Charlie is open to new ideas and ways of thinking, at times in the transcripts it feels as though this may not be the case because of categorical statements that she makes, such as 'I'll never have a good relationship with my mother now; I can't believe anyone really likes me because I'm not the sort of person people like'.

I feel strongly that much of this is to do with Charlie's learned survival patterns and that it is possible to work on changing these. I have confidence that with time and support, Charlie will learn to give herself much more credit for her achievements, and will learn to love and nurture that little girl inside her who so desperately needs to be heard. I have confidence that she could learn to reconcile the two estranged parts of herself – the competent, articulate, organized person in the world of paid work, and the married woman fearful of her husband leaving her, the person who finds it so hard to believe in her loveable nature. The fact that she has rethought some aspects of what she originally said in her reply to my questions is an indication of the possibility for change.

She mentions feminism, although I do not know exactly which aspects of feminism she means; but this suggests that she is interested in exploring political and social influences on women's lives. I want to encourage her to look at all aspects of her life, to value every one of them for what they are worth and not take anything for granted.

Contraindications with Charlie are that her intellectual abilities may get in the way of her dealing with issues on an emotional level – especially as this is one of the ways in which she has survived difficult times. She may want to rationalize away her right to feel pain and anger, and be too nice and understanding. This is a problem many women face, again because of their upbringing stressing roles as caretaker for everyone else's needs. I am concerned that she might see her needs as too trivial to be bothered with and minimize her pain. Such behaviour will only be a shield for dealing with that pain and might help her survive on a superficial basis, but it will not help her deal fundamentally with the hurt and rejection, in a way that could be liberating. There might be some resistance in Charlie to looking at herself in a different way and this could surface both in individual work and in groupwork.

Charlie may find individual work too confrontational. In a group, participants can take it in turns to sit back. The vibrancy that comes through in the transcripts suggests to me that Charlie could derive tremendous benefit and support from a group where there would be laughter and fun as well as tears and distress. Her liveliness would gain a forum for expression and be valued by other women. She would see other women finding ways of dealing with their pain and recognizing and valuing their own and each others' achievements. The power of this cannot be underestimated.

The course of therapy

I want to offer Charlie a contract for a year in the first instance. This will include the possibility of starting with individual therapy on a weekly basis for an hour. There will be the option of participating in a women's group at the point where this is practical and Charlie feels it right for her.

The therapy on an individual basis will involve looking at those areas Charlie wants to discuss, where she feels her strengths lie, looking at what she does in all aspects of her life. I will ask her to think about everything she is involved in, to look at what each of them entails and to recognize and value the complexity of it all. I will encourage her not to take herself for granted. What is expected of her as a woman, and what does she want out of life? We will look at the similarities and differences between these and where they come from: Are they from within her, are they what she sees as society's expectations of her, are they what other people have told her? I will ask her again what images of adult womanhood she absorbed as a young girl, whether this happened in different ways, that is was she *told* how she would be expected to behave as a woman, or did she pick up ideas from observation and listening? Were there consistencies and/or inconsistencies in what she heard?

I will explain to Charlie that feminist therapy as practised by me, both in individual work and in groupwork, is not the same as 'work with women'. It is possible for a therapist to carry out such work without ever engaging in what I consider to be a feminist approach. I want to ensure from the outset that Charlie feels happy with this, otherwise I would not want to continue. My understanding in these circumstances is that the structural influences on her experience will be given their true weight, that Charlie will come to see that she is not to blame for the attitudes of other people towards her, but she will be encouraged to look at what she is proud of in herself. She will also be encouraged to value this and to recognize the interplay of all aspects of herself. I will ask her about her wishes and aspirations and will encourage her to think about stages along the road to reaching these. We will look at how she feels in different circumstances, whether she feels withdrawn, angry, confused. We will explore ways of expressing those feelings and giving them equal value. I want to know whether she still has migraines or any other manifestation of tension. If so, what does she do about this? I want to use some assertiveness techniques, as much as possible in a way that leaves Charlie feeling in control of what is happening in her life.

What does she want? A better relationship with her mother? Not to fear that her husband will walk out? To feel that she makes decisions about her life because *she* wants to, not because of a voice in her head telling her what to do? To be confident in friendships with other people and to have that inherent trust that comes from her own feelings of self-worth? She trusts others' attitudes to herself at work because she knows that her opinions and expertise are valued. I want to enable her to learn to feel that way in more situations. It may be that sometimes she wavers, but it is important that she sees that she is the same person, whatever the circumstances she is in.

In groupwork, I want to look at how the ways in which we have grown up as women differ from what we know was expected of us as children, and what the expectations that we had ourselves were of how things might be. How much can Charlie see that these changes have been brought about by her own actions? I hope that she can learn to be more confident about herself, think about what her own needs are and begin to describe them. This is often very difficult for women. I want also to reframe some of the statements others have used to describe her, or she has described herself, so that these can be made into something more positive. My main concern with Charlie is that her intellect will prevent her from allowing herself to *feel*. I do not mean by this that her intellect should not be valued, quite the contrary. But I want her to be able to recognize *all* aspects of herself as equally valid and equally love-able. I want her to be able to learn to undo the knot that has said only certain bits of her are worthy of others' attention and respect, and that the rest must be frozen away in the iceberg. Also, I want her to learn that it is OK to say no, to say when she can or cannot deal with another person's pain, even if that person is someone very close, such as her husband. He has to take responsibility for himself.

I will ask her to think about what will happen if she *does* say what she thinks on certain situations, expressing anger, rage, disagreement, excitement, happiness – does it mean that people will know what she is thinking, that they will not necessarily be horrified, that people's respect for her might grow, that she might feel more self-respect because she has not been silenced? I want to ask her to think of times when she has been an iceberg. What exactly has happened? What has she wanted to be different? With whom? What does she stand to gain or lose from trying to change this behaviour? Or from leaving things the way they are? I will ask her to think about the fear of trying out new behaviour, and how the fear of doing something is often greater than the actual results of doing it.

Working in a group at a time like this may well be beneficial, as other women will be able to give Charlie support in trying out new ideas. If she feels confident enough, she can role-play a particular scene. This could be with her mother, her husband or anyone else she chooses. It will be for Charlie to decide whether she wants to be herself or to act the other person. Sometimes, acting the other person can provide us with insights into their thoughts and feelings and fears that we could not otherwise imagine. She may well come to realize that the negative feelings she thought she inspired are not there at all.

I want to contact the little girl inside Charlie, recognizing and validating the playfulness, vulnerability and determination of this person. I want to demonstrate to Charlie how this person has grown up, which parts of her have been encouraged and which have been stifled. We will look at how this has happened and learn which lessons can be used to maintain and increase Charlie's self-awareness and self-confidence.

In relation to Charlie's abortion, I want to use the group experience again to demonstrate to her that such events occur frequently in women's lives, often with no appropriate support. I hope that the group's response will go some way towards redressing this and give her credit for the action she took.

An issue which needs considerable exploration, and which for Charlie might feel safer in individual work, is the connection between the abortion she had and the fact that her mother told her that if abortion had been available when she herself was pregnant, Charlie might never have been born. Such a statement is indeed devastating and it is vital that Charlie is given as much support as possible to recognize the very different circumstances that led her to make the decision about her baby. It is very difficult to lay down the burden of guilt about this child's life, but I want to encourage Charlie to see that she made the decision because of her love for children and her sense of connectedness through the birth process. It is important, too, that she values the love and respect that she has from other people now, as a means of easing the anger and rejection she feels about her mother's statement. Just as important to celebrate is her keeping alive her baby's memory.

Problem areas

The problems I foresee with Charlie are that her intellect may function at the expense of her emotions because she has not been able to trust her self-expression for so long. It is also possible that she may decide she does not want to participate in a group. She may see this as far too threatening, and/or inappropriate for her because she may not feel safe with other women. It seems likely that Charlie will want to continue with individual work because of the amount already apparent in the transcripts, but this is no guarantee of feeling safe in groupwork. I feel very strongly that if Charlie *could* become involved in a sympathetic and supportive group, this would be immensely valuable to her. At the same time, it has to be her decision and this in itself is part of getting away from doing things because other people tell her she should. Overcoming the embarrassment she might feel about being involved in a group is one of the difficulties I foresee, but the very act of involvement could be just what she needs. It will give her solidarity, scope to believe in herself, constant reinforcement of her qualities and skills, the chance to practise making positive statements about herself, the chance to hear other women make positive statements about her, the right to say things about other women, the opportunity to learn that we all have different aspects of ourselves that people like and respect and want to know more of – so that she can begin to think less that she is 'not the sort of person other people like'. She can choose how to introduce herself to people for the very first time, naming qualities or skills that she feels she has. I hope this will lead on to looking at the fact that she can decide how she wants others to perceive her and that this can be positive, and that if she projects a positive image, she may find herself living up to this, she may enjoy and appreciate the responses she gets to this behaviour. This in turn can lead to her making more effort to act in a way that gives her the type of attention she wants. Eventually, this may lead to her having far less room for self-doubt. My concern about this not succeeding stems from the categorical statements Charlie made in the transcripts – they leave me feeling that she is scared about making changes in case they do not work. I think that intellectually she may well say that she wants things to be different, but that emotionally it is too big a step to take and she is concerned about the risk involved. Another concern I have is that Charlie may be resistant to seeing certain aspects of her mother's behaviour in a different, more positive, light. I think it will be hard to encourage Charlie to differentiate those elements of past experience that have shaped her current behaviour and thoughts, and those for which she can recognize responsibility herself. Any discussion on these issues would not be an attempt to trivialize or reframe the impact her mother's behaviour had and still has on Charlie's self-image; rather, it would be an attempt to unlock the aspects of Charlie that are intrinsically *her*, of which she can be proud, and which she can nurture.

I will look at words Charlie uses to describe herself and her behaviour and work on finding as many ways as possible to make these positive. This will involve reframing, an element of feminist therapy which can be both liberating or threatening depending on many factors. Reframing involves reinterpreting descriptions frequently used of a person in a positive and not derogatory light, for example seeing 'stubbornness' as determination, 'frozenness' as self-protection, 'watchfulness' as acute observation and perceptiveness, 'selfishness' as legitimate self-nurturing. Reframing can provide an entirely new perspective on life, can encourage a change in thought patterns, or it can lead to virtual disintegration of the self-image a person has built up and carried around over the years. Such an approach needs to be used with great care and taken very much at the pace of the individual. It can lead to sudden revelations and insights about what appear to be entrenched behaviours. These revelations may not always be welcome, but they may enable a person to reappraise her actions in a more self-affirmative light. My concern with Charlie is that she sometimes gives the impression of having become so fixed in her image of herself as controlled by her mother other than in very specific circumstances, that she is unwilling to lose this image because it is familiar. What I feel unsure about is her willingness to realize that she is responsible for her own happiness, that her concern about whether other people like her or not is more likely to hinder the establishment of relationships rather than foster them, and that learning to be more relaxed will encourage her to be open – will melt the iceberg a little, and she will very probably find that people will respond positively to her. I am concerned that letting go of some of her survival mechanisms may feel too threatening because the picture she will end up drawing of herself will be so different from the one she knows. She may find it hard to believe in and accept the changes.

This could mean only partial success in the therapeutic outcome. I hope it will not, because, fundamentally, I believe that Charlie's intelligence and need for approval could work together to create an image of herself with which she felt happy. But as her therapist, I would need to be on the look-out for these issues all the time. I feel it is important that Charlie finds ways of recognizing her emotional connections with other women and the strength and solidarity to be gained from this. If the wounds left by the rejection she felt as a child can become scars and not remain open, then I feel this is possible. All the while they remain wounds, it is as if the negative influence from her mother still holds sway and the pain she feels in this unloving connection prevents her from risking the formation of other links. I hope that if Charlie learns to enter into friendships with other women that do not feel as 'controlled' by her mother's presence as before, then her relationship with her mother itself may improve.

Criteria for successful outcome

The criteria that I have for success in this case are as follows. At the outset I will ask Charlie to draw a picture – in whichever way makes sense for her (i.e. literally drawing, describing, using collage, etc.) – of her wishes and aspirations. I will encourage her to take the work we do in stages and not to feel that she has to achieve major changes all at once. If she wishes, I will offer her the option of a regular review of not only which issues we have covered or are covering, but of how she is thinking and feeling. I am wary of using words like 'success' because of the goal-oriented approach it can imply. I would like Charlie to feel as much as possible that she is in control of whatever process of change is occurring and that standards of measurement are her own. Clearly, there are more objective criteria that one can set as a therapist, but for me there has to be as much flexibility as possible and it has to be on Charlie's own terms. It is important that she achieves what she feels is right for her and that it is not anyone else's imposition. I feel very strongly that this is a major element of feminist approaches to counselling and therapy. It is *not* non-directive counselling, because the client is encouraged to look at different factors in her life which have contributed to her state of mind and to work out where she can take control of the effects of these. It may be that what she says she wants to look at at the outset may be totally different from what is eventually discussed. Again, this is her decision, but I will ask periodically if she wants to return to a particular area of discussion that had been raised before and then left. I hope it will be possible to do this without her feeling under pressure. I am confident that Charlie will benefit from my brand of feminist approach to therapy, but I am less confident about predicting to what extent. Looking at the world from any feminist perspective, whether it be radical, separatist, socialist or whatever, will have its impact. If Charlie feels that this approach to the world speaks to her, then it is very likely that she will see other aspects of her life differently too. She will need to define where her support systems are, whether her marriage and established friendships will be enhanced or challenged by any changes in thinking that she undergoes. It is hard to go back to where you were once a different view has been found that makes sense.

Bearing in mind my areas of concern described above, if Charlie reaches the point where she feels able to join a group that would inevitably be supportive (because of its ground rules, support in discussion, other women's experiences, hearing other women including me say positive things about her, etc.), then I believe that 'success' is a possibility.

My confidence is based on the number of women I have worked with over the years, individually and in groups, where the most amazing voyages of change and self-discovery have taken place. Where a woman is prepared to take the risk of re-appraising her survival strategies, then untold benefit can be derived. This comes in the form of feeling more relaxed, recognizing the limits of personal responsibility, feeling greater self-worth, making clear statements about personal aspirations, having more self-confidence, forming alliances with other women, seeing women as surviving and resisting in a society that does little to promote well-being, valuing the diversity and differences between women, recognizing self-doubt as an integral part of human reaction, but not seeing it as categorical and having to overshadow everything else in life.

It will be for Charlie to decide when she feels she has reached a stage in the therapeutic process where she wants to stop. At that point, I will ask her to paint a picture of herself again and compare this with the one she produced at the beginning, and any others that she has put together along the way. In my experience, the very fact of taking time, of unlearning to apologize for everything she says or thinks, of unlearning phrases such as, 'Well, I don't suppose you'll think this is that important, it's just a little thought I had', and many others of that nature, can give women the opportunity to examine exactly what they *do* think and feel. They can then interpret themselves in their own way, and not feel they have to accept the rewriting and trivializing of their own experience that so many others may try to offer them. These reactions are so often born of the disbelief and impatience of other people, as well as the difficulties they may have in facing their own pain, rekindled by listening to other women's experiences. While not seeking to criticize the silencing behaviour of others, because this will so often be done for reasons they possibly cannot help, there is no doubt that the effects of this are damaging and long-lasting. A feminist approach enables a woman to see the structural and socio-political reasons behind her and others' behaviour and to learn ways of taking as much control as possible in her own life.

Summary

I think that Charlie will benefit from work in an all-woman and woman-centred environment. I think she needs positive reinforcement herself, she needs positive images of women and she needs as much nurturing as possible. She needs help to name and confront her fears, to name and celebrate her triumphs, to learn to unfreeze her emotions and have some fun, to allow herself to get in touch with her needy but also creative child. She needs loving and validation, massage, healing, respect, love, admiration for the way in which she keeps alive the spirit of her dead baby. She needs help looking at all the things that she sees already as positive about herself. She needs to know that taking care of herself involves all different aspects of behaviour – and that it is not spoiling herself. She needs to unlearn guilt. She needs to put her well-developed political awareness to good use in understanding that she cannot possibly be to blame for all the things her mother accused her of – responsibility for her father's death, and getting away with it because her sister and not herself is ill now.

I see Charlie as a woman wanting all these things and finding it very difficult to believe that she even has the right to want them, let alone *have* them. I am reasonably confident that work with her on her own and in a group will provide her with both the belief in the right to have needs, and the belief in the right to learn how to meet them. This self-validation will, I hope, diminish her feelings of low self-esteem and incredulity that anyone could like her. From reading the transcript and her replies to my questions, I see her as someone with whom it would be a tremendous pleasure to work.

Further reading

Butler, S. and Wintram, C. (1993). *Feminist Groupwork*. London: Sage.
Dickson, A. (1992). *A Woman in Your Own Right: Assertiveness and You*. London: Quartet.
Ernst, S. and Goodison, L. (1992). *In Our Own Hands: A Book of Self-Help Therapy*. London: Women's Press.
Ernst, S. and Maguire, M. (Eds) (1987). *Living with the Sphinx: Papers from the Women's Therapy Centre*. London: Women's Press.
Orbach, S. and Eichenbaum, L. (1987). *Bittersweet*. London: Arrow.

MICHAEL JACOBS AND CHARLIE

REVIEW AND RESPONSE

Charlie and I met after reading each of the therapist's contributions. It was nearly two years after the first interview, and I was anxious about the effect of the process on her. My guess was that she would have been very absorbed in reading and in thinking about the various accounts based on our initial and subsequent interviews. I feared, as indeed a few of the therapists also hinted, that she might have been hurt by some of the interpretations that had been made of her. Despite my re-iterated offer of support in many of the letters I had sent her I had heard nothing, and I approached the final interview with a mixture of excitement and anxiousness.

Charlie had valued all the contributions. She said at first that she had not found the process threatening or upsetting, although she later indicated places where she had found a deeper sadness and fear within herself. She described how she had found herself reading about Charlie as though Charlie was someone else: this was partly because the change of her real name had had this effect, but perhaps it was partly because she was reading about the child in herself. Just as Phil Lapworth said in his contribution that he found himself wanting to be a father to Charlie, on reading the material she had found herself 'wanting to mother myself, if you see what I mean. I wanted to put my arms round her and say "There, there" . . .'. She wanted to give herself the mothering she could not get when she was younger.

The chapters and the transcripts were all neatly filed in her ring binder which could scarcely contain all the pages. In our meeting we were both surrounded by our papers, and as the interview went on these papers spread around us over the floor, reminiscent of a description Charlie had given in one of her answers to Cassie Cooper. She told her how she left all the newspapers scattered across the front room floor and thought, 'I really ought to tidy this room up. I thought, "My mother would want me to do that. Sod it – I'm going to bed".' Clearly, in our case, all this paper was a rich mine of hypothesis and response which Charlie had not been afraid to dig into, and which we could never 'tidy up' neatly. There was so much to comment upon. What I record here is a digest of our individual responses, although the reader is bound to have made other observations about similarities and differences between these therapists. Some readers may even have seen areas which none of us have identified to date.

Charlie's assessment of each therapist was a balance of appreciation, of thoughtfulness and of criticism of a detail here or there. She described how what she had tried to do when she was reading each chapter was to imagine that the therapist was talking to her, and how she would like to have replied (as she does here) to some of their further thoughts, as well as to those ideas where she disagreed.

We talked for two hours. As in the first interview we quickly got into the different issues, and her feelings were openly expressed. Charlie was not afraid to reveal more about herself, including a little of the dream she could not tell Alix Pirani in the second set of interviews. What was different about her now was that there were far fewer of the apologetic put-downs of herself which had been obvious from the opening sentence on the occasion when we had initially met. She had noticed herself, when she read the first transcript, how she kept saying she was sorry, and she had made a conscious effort ever since not to do this. This was one of a number of ways she had changed, which she attributed to taking part in this process. There was still much she wished to explore within herself, as became clear, but there was a confidence about her self-worth which it turned out each of the therapists had in their own way helped her to develop.

Cassie Cooper

Although this contribution appears first in this book, when we met Charlie wanted to leave her comments on Cassie Cooper's chapter until last. It was clearly the most difficult one for her to absorb. She had found what Cooper wrote about the Kleinian model of development 'extremely pessimistic'. The feeling she got reading it was, 'This is so sad. And I wasn't sure whether this was my sadness, or her sadness, or both of us'. She found the chapter 'very, very different from the others'. Like the other contributions, it was written not for Charlie herself, but for the discerning therapist, and therefore it contained technical language. Charlie found some of this language more difficult to understand than in other therapies (although transactional analysis presented her with a similar problem).

It is perhaps one of the difficulties of Kleinian theory that it uses terms which do not mean all that they appear to: 'the depressive position' is a clear example of this. To the lay person, this looks uncannily like depression, and therefore carries a negative connotation. For Kleinians, of course, the depressive position is a sign of maturing, and of a degree of resolution of earlier paranoid difficulties. Although Charlie was puzzled by some of this terminology, she understood it a little better when it was linked to herself. She 'turned the page and it was there: oh! Is that really me?' But she found some of the descriptions hard to accept. I had myself anticipated that there might be this type of confusion over the phrase in Cassie Cooper's chapter, 'sadistic envious feelings towards her sister'. Charlie could not at first accept the possibility of such feelings. She then thought hard about it and thought 'Perhaps I do' and began 'to feel very guilty about it, and what I don't need is yet more guilt'. She tried to deny she had any *sadistic* envy, but she acknowledged that when she thought about her sister she was very judgemental. In her answer to one of the questions, she had also seen how judgemental she was of her sister, and recognized for the first time just how critical of her she can be. This, she thought, confirmed her envy of her sister. Yet in comparison with her sister's illness, Charlie felt very lucky. She also feels very compassionate to her sister, but without any kind of emotional involvement. But she still found the sadistic part of the phrase impossible to understand.

I suggested that if we saw some of the punitive feelings involved in her criticism of her sister, they could be described as 'a sort of sadism', and this made a little more sense to her. 'Sadism' has a much wider and universal meaning in Kleinian theory than it does in everyday conversation, where it is reserved for a particular type of vicious pleasure in cruelty. Although Cooper's phrase had not been all that helpful, it had opened up a whole new area, and was clearly worth Charlie thinking about more, although she thought she was 'not yet ready for it'. And if the 'sadism' felt a little hard to swallow (if I can use a further Kleinian metaphor!), others (Ryle, Pirani and Margison) also pick up the envy in the material in the first session, even if they do not interpret it in quite the same way, as I draw out below.

What Cassie Cooper does is to explore the implications of Charlie's inner world, and I find she does this in a way which is different from any of the other therapists. It appears at times dispassionate, pure analysis, although what she deduces certainly gave rise to all sorts of emotions, perhaps in the reader, certainly in Charlie and myself. Cooper more frequently gets hold of what might indeed be called the darker, more negative side of Charlie's experience. Charlie's being sent away to London after her father's death, for example, although it seems from all she says to have been a good experience, also involved being sent away soon after her sister was born, another example of being 'got rid of', as Cassie Cooper graphically expresses it.

Her questions to Charlie concentrated on her very early years. If there is less mention of Charlie's positive achievements than in the other therapists' accounts, it is perhaps because she did not ask about these either. She did not ask, for example, about Charlie's own mothering of her children, as others did and therefore misses out on some of the 'good bits', which Charlie thought were missing from Cooper's account. It was the most upsetting of the chapters for her, although Charlie commented 'she seemed to care about me as well'. We both noted the real concern for Charlie in the last few paragraphs. Cassie Cooper kept returning to the artificiality of the situation of being involved in this project. And although the other therapists also mentioned this, she expressed it as a real sense of loss, of missing something through not meeting Charlie, and this had impressed Charlie: 'In reflecting my losses, and relating them to her loss of me, she is reflecting it back to me in a very powerful sort of way. She mentions her difficulty of letting go, almost as if she found it difficult to let go of me, just as I find it hard to let go of my anger'. I, too, had thought that it was difficult for Charlie to stay with her anger for long. Although Cooper's analysis made sense of the splitting in the first interview between Charlie's mother as being very bad for the way she had treated Charlie, or very good for having coped with all that had happened, the latter sense of making reparation to her mother always seemed to me to be expressed too rapidly, before the real fury with her mother had been worked through.

Cassie Cooper invited Charlie to communicate with her: 'I want her to know that should she wish to communicate with me, I will be pleased to hear from her. It is a better ending than to write Charlie off'. Charlie was not sure at this stage of what she could say. She also thought that it was as yet too soon to say what her response to this chapter was. She imagined that she would in time come back to it, and find it helpful. That is my impression too. I guess that Cassie Cooper reveals her thinking to Charlie earlier than she would have had Charlie been her client. Over a period of time, what appears at first glance to be a more critical analysis may prove to be less judgemental and guilt-provoking, and more understanding of the complex feelings present in Charlie's presentation. Certainly, Charlie was recognizing as a result of all the contributions the possibility of much deeper feelings than she had yet got in touch with.

Phil Lapworth

As with Kleinian terminology, Charlie had found three phrases in the transactional analysis of her particularly difficult to understand: one (in fact not particularly related to therapy at all) was 'phenomenological' (referring to the study of what 'appears' rather than what necessarily 'is'). The other two were 'pure' transactional analysis. One was 'rackets' (which Lapworth does describe as 'a feeling substituted for the original feelings that were not allowed expression in childhood'), and the other was 'a Type 3 impasse' (which he illustrates as 'I have always been like this, this is really me, I can't be otherwise'). The reader needs to remember that each of the therapists was writing for a therapeutically informed readership, and that such technical language might not be used with the client without further explanation. Charlie was in a unique position, of reading, as it were, her therapist's notes. Nevertheless, it is one of the most immediate impressions of transactional analysis on the outsider, that it tends to use a large number of 'jargon' phrases. Far from being simplistic (as Phil Lapworth recognizes some people say of transactional analysis), it is extremely complex. The terms used are often in what is deceptively simple language, but the common words and phrases used (like 'racket') are not so straightforward in their meaning. It is definitely a language which has to be learned to be properly used.

Most of what Charlie had heard previously about transactional analysis was from other people, and 'a bit negative'. In fact, she found she 'quite warmed to him in a way that surprised me'. She particularly valued Lapworth's summaries under *child feelings, child thoughts* and *child behaviours*. She was aware that the therapist was quoting here from her own words, but the way in which he had put it all together had a powerful effect on her. It was very accurate: 'that's me'. She liked the way he had said, 'Charlie is doing all she can already, and what she must avoid is downplaying my own way of coming to terms with it' (as she put it to me). She felt that Phil Lapworth was very perceptive. He was very optimistic about the outcome, which made her feel optimistic about it too. She had noted that he liked her, and she had liked him even before she realized his feelings towards her. She appreciated the way he acknowledged that it would be easy for him to try to replace her father, but that this would be 'a cop-out'. (Ryle saw the transference/counter-transference relationship more in terms of her grandfather, perhaps reflecting in each case the age of the therapist.) She noted that Lapworth really admired the way she tried to survive. Yet Charlie went on to question why she needed him to like her. She recognized that she had a need for re-assurance – a need for people to like her before she could respond to them.

Phil Lapworth's speculation about the meaning of the story of Robin Hood to her was perhaps superfluous: 'I just liked it because it was an exciting story!' But he was 'dead right' when he speculated about what Maid Marion meant for her: 'bravery, courage, rebellion, excitement and caring'. Charlie noted that her reply to a similar question asked by Margison, that she saw herself as Hamlet, was a description of herself as she is; Maid Marion is the person she would like to be, her ideal.

One of Lapworth's concerns is that Charlie might act out by ending therapy. She herself felt that this was not correct. For her to get upset and to walk out is something she could never do. She would always end therapy by mutual agreement.

Charlie and I had had the advantage of working through all six sets of questions. Our own information was therefore fuller than any of the individual therapist's pictures could have been. This leads to some interesting comparisons and contrasts in the questions asked and the answers given. Among the answers to Phil Lapworth's set of questions was a fascinating confirmation of one of the questions put to me by Pirani. She had asked at what age I saw Charlie as being. I replied to her, before asking Charlie Lapworth's question about what brought Charlie to therapy at this particular time, that my first and most immediate thought was 'thirteen'; but because my intellect then rubbished that answer, I adapted my answer to 'seventeen', finally compromising on fifteen. My original, 'top-of-the-head' reply proved to be the accurate one, because Charlie said to Lapworth's query about why she was coming now, that it was because her daughter, then aged thirteen, had led Charlie to compare herself with her: 'I think seeing her growing up and seeing how differently from me she's turned out made me aware that I wasn't really coping as well as I thought I was'. It was a remarkable confirmation of the significance of the age thirteen, which neither therapist could know at that time because of their separate knowledge.

At the same time, the reader will have seen that the six therapists emphasize different parallels of Charlie's current issues with past developmental stages. Cassie Cooper concentrates on the years three to six. Phil Lapworth sees the adolescent issues as important, not surprisingly when the precipitating factor given in answer to his question is her daughter being thirteen. Claire Wintram picks up on the abortion as a central issue, and the tenth anniversary of it coinciding with her presenting herself for therapy – as perhaps Charlie's description of the deep depression following the first interview confirms. Frank Margison thinks both the anniversary of the abortion and her daughter's adolescence are possible precipitating factors. Phil Lapworth and Alix Pirani choose not to refer to the abortion of Charlie's child at all, and Anthony Ryle only makes one brief reference to 'the terminated pregnancy' in his reformulation letter.

Other differences between the therapists also become apparent. Phil Lapworth's question about the happiest occasion of Charlie's life elicits the straight and simple response 'the birth of my three children'. And to Pirani she used the phrase 'post-natal euphoria' to describe her response to her children's birth. But while Cassie Cooper acknowledges in one of her questions the many positive things in Charlie's adult life ('marriage, children, friendship, work'), she also suggests that Charlie 'barely touched upon' her own mothering in her account, and quotes by contrast Berke's delight in his son. Much again depends on the questions a therapist asks.

Phil Lapworth was less informed by Charlie's response to the question he asked about how he and Charlie would know they had achieved her therapeutic goal, and what would be different for her. This drew no response! He acknowledges the need to explain the reason for the question; but it is worth noting how Margison's follow-up to the same initial question elicited a much fuller response. Drawing upon Charlie's considerable ability to use her imagination, he put this supplementary question to her: 'Try to imagine yourself waking up: how do you know things have changed? Take me through a typical day, still imagining that you have already changed, and tell me what is different as you meet different people'. Margison comments in his chapter that her response is detailed and 'gives me confidence that we could work on agreed goals and also know when we had achieved them'. His question is a useful model which other therapists might learn from.

Lapworth and Margison both asked a number of questions about Charlie's attitude to therapy itself. In this they differ from the other therapists who took her motivation for granted, presumably as a result of the very full first interview. Ryle clearly felt that the first interview 'suggested that she had pre-existing ideas about therapy and that she was basically capable of trust'.

Charlie's principal reservation about her transactional analysis therapist was 'whether he really could help me to stop feeling the impasse' (which she appears to have understood after all) that 'I have always been like this, this is really me, I can't be otherwise'.

Many of his insights were very helpful, but he seemed to expect Charlie to be able to do a lot of work: consciously she was prepared to do this, but she wondered whether she actually had the capacity to change that type of thinking: 'I wouldn't want to let him down', she added. I suggested to her that this latter fear may be an example of transference to the therapist of her anxiety about letting her mother down. Phil Lapworth also recognizes this area of the transference relationship: 'there is the potential problem of Charlie seeing me as a critical Parent who (like mother) is impossible to please'.

Frank Margison

Charlie felt Margison's chapter was easy to understand. He also said that she was likely to benefit from any kind of therapy, and again, as with Lapworth, she liked that kind of optimism. Margison's reference to brief therapy puzzled her: was this because he worked in the NHS and this was all he could offer? Or was this a treatment of choice? In fact it is interesting that Ryle, now retired from an NHS post, and in another volume in the series, a clinical psychologist working in the NHS, also suggest the possibilities that could accrue from brief therapy, reflecting perhaps the pressures on the NHS psychotherapy services. Cooper also refers to brief therapy, perhaps unusual in a Kleinian, although her own recent work setting of student counselling also has to face a similar level of demand to the NHS.

Because Frank Margison was a representative of psychoanalytic psychotherapy, Charlie was not expecting any hint of briefer work. She had the image of analysis as lasting for several years. The possibility of brief therapy again made her feel optimistic. She also feels comfortable in the NHS environment, since she knows a number of people who work in that context: 'You know what to expect when you go into hospital or you go to your GP. Although it may be scary it's not a totally unfamiliar context'.

The questions he asked about whom she would like to work with, the gender and type of therapy, were unique to this sample of therapists – perhaps because Margison saw this as a real assessment in an NHS context, rather than as the start of ongoing therapy with him. Charlie imagined, when the questions had originally been asked (since the sources of all the questions were not identified), that it was a feminist therapist asking them: she could see this was her own stereotyping of therapists.

Frank Margison's comment on the results of the Symptom Check-list, that her 'depression is not severe but it is pervasive' is, Charlie felt, not accurate but an understandable interpretation of her. This is because she describes herself as 'a bit miserable', even when she is desperately depressed. She loses the strength of her feelings at such times: it is 'a feeling of no feelings', as she put it.

Yet another of Margison's comments hinted that 'she might find more than she bargained for'. Charlie also wondered whether she would find something in therapy that she could not deal with. I asked her whether in terms of the whole process she had found more than she bargained for? She thought not, although she admitted that the death of her father, and her feelings towards her mother, might contain more than she had yet realized. She could remember much around that time of her father's death, such as the presents she had for her fifth birthday, and the year in London. But she could not remember him dying or being told that he had died, or the funeral, or anything about it at all. 'Clearly it must be there somewhere, and I've repressed it'. Cassie Cooper and Alix Pirani had suggested that she had never been allowed to grieve for her father, and this Charlie felt was correct. Her mother, when anything had happened, always said 'You must put it behind you' rather than 'You must come to terms with it'. Charlie assumed that she had told her in such a way that Charlie could not cry. She was afraid that the feelings would come through, and the pain would be absolutely terrifying. She knew, from the death of her grandfather, how painful grief can be, and she was concerned that the pain over the death of her father might be even worse. But although Charlie said all this in response to my choosing to highlight Frank Margison's sugges-tion that she might in therapy find 'more than she bargained for', it is interesting that he did not himself identify the death of her father as one of his core issues.

Similarly, her feelings about her mother: Wintram hints that in a group of other women Charlie would learn sympathy for her mother (which Charlie and I felt she was all too ready to express in the first interview). She does appreciate her mother's struggle, and all that her mother had to cope with. But she could still not forgive it – and as she said this she realized how worked up she was becoming. Charlie felt she was not good at expressing anger. Margison had wondered whether she would be able to express this towards her therapist. She knew that one of the things that scared her was that if she were to go into her childhood, and try to relive the feelings then, she might get so angry that it would be embarrassing and is frightening to have such feelings. There was indeed the possibility of 'more than she bargained for'.

Charlie thought that Frank Margison's list of the metaphors he identified in her material was good. He singled out her key conflicts as autonomy, worth and sexuality. The first two made much sense to her, although she felt sexuality was not such an issue, because she enjoyed sex, except when she was depressed. She acknowledged it was an issue in her adolescence, and now in that she has teenage children, but mainly because of the AIDS scare.

Margison, like Cooper, Pirani and Ryle, identifies envy as one of the main facets in Charlie's account. He differs, however, from Cooper, stressing more her mother's envy of Charlie's 'growth, intellect and sexuality', whereas Cooper stresses Charlie's envy of her sister. Pirani suggests that Charlie's dying father may have been 'envious of her very being', and the 'envious, poisonous' mother's breast as one of Charlie's projections. Margison describes how 'Charlie can only escape through "identification with the aggressor"', suggesting that she also has her own envy to contend with. It is interesting to note the subtle differences in Margison, Pirani and Cooper on envy, two of them representing different wings of Object Relations Theory, with Pirani clearly having also studied it. Both Margison and Cooper agree in identifying the difficulties caused for Charlie by not having a father as an escape route. Had her father survived, she would have had someone closer than her grandfather could be as a buffer against her mother. Even her grandfather died when things were getting difficult again in her teens. At two key points in her life, when she was five years old and sixteen years old, she lost a highly significant male figure.

Other similarities and differences between Frank Margison and the other therapists have been alluded to above, and are taken up further below: his perception of metaphor, his use of fictional characters that she identified with, his question about outcome, his interpretation of the cornet dream, and his reservation about suggesting group therapy. What is distinctive about his chapter is that he is the only therapist to take up the significance of my own relationship with Charlie. He picks up the transference implications of my meeting her with her husband in another setting, where us both knowing her so well gave rise to strong feelings in her. Margison sees how this whole project of working with the client and six therapists is not unlike therapy itself, and that the editor in each case becomes a key transference figure to the client.

Finally, Charlie liked Frank Margison's reference to Radclyffe Hall's book, and the parallels with herself. She was looking for it, to be able to read it, although she was less sure about reading a suggestion put to her by Pirani, in a private communication that is not included in her chapter, of returning to D.H. Lawrence.

Alix Pirani

Charlie explained that this contribution 'made me think an awful lot'. She had read in the field of mythology herself, and had become quite interested in Jung. She did not find Pirani's chapter as immediately reassuring as either Lapworth's or Ryle's, although she had then asked herself why she needed to be reassured. Alix Pirani presented her with many insights. Her analysis of Charlie's cornet dream felt right: 'the nightmare is of her own inner little girl's loss of the potent harmonizing male – the man out there or the masculine within in the context of mother's unworthiness and inability to hold him, or the masculine principle, for her'. Yet she also thought Margison's different interpretation of the same dream was right: his tentative thought included identification of her daughter's creativity (and the threat of its loss) with her own 'lost childhood'. And a disguised, possibly aggressive aspect of the dream: anxiety about restricting her daughter's creativity, and possibly identification with her mother who restricted Charlie's own creativity and ability 'to play'. Two very different interpretations, each of which she found helpful, was very confusing!

As we discussed Alix Pirani's chapter, Charlie was able to say more about her 'unmentionable dream', which she could not tell her about the first time. It was perhaps a sign of her growing confidence at looking at herself more deeply, and a response to Pirani's graphic use of images. The main image in this dream had been a well, 'which is a very female image, and it was the well which frightened me'. She thought she was scared about female power, not just in authoritative women, but also in herself as well.

Charlie also thought it was right that she needed to explore and honour her Celtic roots. She felt alienated from her Welsh forebears, although she was not sure how she would go about making this connection. She hastened to add that she did not feel attracted to paganism in a religious way. Alix Pirani was the only therapist who picked up (as it turned out a little mistakenly) the reference to the pastoral connection in Charlie's husband. She also recognized the experience of St Paul's Cathedral when Charlie was five. She had asked about Charlie's relationship to the Church. Her references to Charlie's 'male God whose church seems empty to her', and the churches' attitude to women, were both ones which Charlie felt strongly. She was impressed by the term 'the dark goddess that has taken hold of Charlie's psyche'. She was caught up in much of the imagery which Pirani used. I wondered whether the images gave rise to intellectual insights alone, or whether they had emotional impact

as well. Charlie's response was that the langu
witches and so on 'felt right'.

Alix Pirani was concerned lest she abuse Charlie a
her interpretations. 'No, not at all', replied Charlie.
could trust her. She felt 'understood and empathized with
not experience Pirani as projecting any of her own feelings
her. She was repeating back to Charlie things that were there a
that Charlie was not conscious of. I asked Charlie whether it made
a difference when she read that Alix Pirani, too, had felt she was not
wanted as a child. Charlie very expressively said, 'Yes it did'. While
she did not feel that Alix Pirani over-identified with her, her sharing
of her own experiences with Charlie helped Charlie to feel that in
many ways Pirani understood her better. She was impressed that she
did not want to break up Charlie's marriage with her envy. She
found the whole chapter 'exciting'.

I noted that Pirani had said that Charlie's language was 'relatively
lacking in metaphor', whereas Margison had described her account
as 'rich in metaphor'. Charlie had noticed the same discrepancy,
and 'was a bit miffed' about Alix Pirani's comment. I have already
noted that other therapists had related Charlie's current difficulties
to her early years, to her adolescence, and to the abortion ten years
ago. Pirani saw Charlie's issues as a mid-life crisis. 'It could be',
thought Charlie, but she added that this was 'a few years off yet',
since her younger child would still be with her for eight or nine
years.

Alix Pirani was the only therapist who asked me for my reactions
to Charlie. This put me in a strange position. Just as Pirani shared
something of herself with Charlie, so she 'made' me reveal something of myself in relation to Charlie through recording my answers
(which I had agreed she could do). I was put in a similar position
to the other therapists, who had said things that they might not
have done so early in a therapeutic relationship, if at all. But I was
the only one who had to meet her face to face, having said these
things. My answers had given Alix Pirani more immediate experience of Charlie. But what was Charlie's reaction to me placing
her age as 'thirteen' or describing her mannerisms. When I asked
Charlie for her reactions to what I had told this therapist, she
replied, 'I was absolutely fascinated. "Oh he's said something
about me!" My husband came into the kitchen and said "What . . . ?",
and I said I was just reading something'. It is interesting not only
that to be noticed by me, and to have made an impression on me,
gives Charlie real sense of value, but that once again, as Margison
picked up with reference to my meeting her elsewhere, her husband

ationship, perhaps again feeling
how her husband had reacted to
eft out, and she had in the end
they had talked about together

ad found my reference to her 'age'
o stop biting her nails (and this was
hat I had said, and if anything was
. The only part that concerned her
e feel 'a bit anxious' and she was

ani got 'completely wrong', to use
Charlie's words, was the reference to Margaret Thatcher 'making
her despair and lose hope in the socialism which is her patriarchal
religion'. She acknowledged that Thatcher was a problem for femin-
ists, but not such a problem for socialist feminist women. Although
Thatcher denied many feminine qualities, this is not a problem,
because as a socialist she believed that class needs to be taken into
account as much as gender. Charlie had more in common with her
working-class brothers than with many upper-class women. She also
still believes in socialism and is 'still there working for it, and one
day . . .'.

Anthony Ryle

Charlie had not heard of cognitive-analytic therapy, and 'objec-
tively found it very interesting'. Once again she appreciated both
Ryle's 'being nice to me', and also his articulation of feelings that
she had never put into words: ' "The main things I pick up from
your story are loss, rejection and survival . . .". "Survival" hadn't
occurred to me before . . . It's so obvious but I hadn't considered it'.
She also liked his sense of humour, citing as an example, 'Charlie
predictably was happy to cooperate with his plan'; and he also referred to her comment in her diary she wrote for him on how
boring it was.

The letter which Anthony Ryle wrote to her at an initial stage,
part of his therapeutic approach, made quite an impact upon me
when I read it to Charlie. It felt a deeply sensitive piece of writing,
really engaging with what Charlie had described. She too experienced it that way, and added, 'I found all of his contribution moved
me in an emotional way'. This was an interesting response to an
approach which lays stress on the cognitive, normally associated as
being the opposite of emotion. Ryle identified crucial issues for her,

including the positive, such as 'your grand old grandfather'. She liked very much the way he said that she had kept her grandfather alive in her – she was pleased that he had seen that because that was what she liked to think was true. Charlie was especially taken with the second letter, and her reaction to his description of 'that part of you which will dismantle what we do, because it is what you want and need'. Initially, she disagreed with this, but then thought about it and recognized that he was right. This had been an important insight for her, partly because she had seen what he described in action, in her initial rejection of what he had said.

There was one correction she wanted to make: the reference to being depressed when her friend had puerperal psychosis, a depression she had described as 'wrong', was not wrong because it was a wrong reaction to have, but because it was the wrong word to use to describe her reaction – she should have said 'sad' about her response to her friend's condition.

Charlie was attracted by the idea of sixteen-session therapy, since it implied that she could change in four months. She was not sure whether she could cope with the homework, or whether she could change in the time available – here her doubts were similar to those she had entertained in respect of Lapworth's optimism. It was not that she would be unwilling to do the work, but that she felt it would not be that successful.

Claire Wintram

'In many ways this was the one I thought I should be keenest on, and in many ways it was'. So Charlie began her review of feminist group therapy. She had noted with approval that Claire Wintram had described her as 'very hard on herself' and that 'it would be a pleasure to work with her'.

What Charlie was more concerned about was that this therapist thought she should get involved in women's groupwork. In some ways it was attractive, and Charlie could see the support she could get from a women's group. But she also felt it was 'scary'. It was one thing to talk about herself to one person, and another to talk to a number of people in a group. Although Claire Wintram said it would be Charlie's decision, she would not know how to decide: she would not know what a group was like until she had tried it, and she could not try it until she had decided to do so. This presented her with an impasse, which she did not know how to cope with. She would like to try, but again Charlie was not clear whether in saying this she just wanted to please the therapist.

I asked Charlie whether the reservations Wintram had described in the opening sentences of the section 'Problem Areas' were accurate: 'too threatening . . . may not feel safe with other women . . . overcoming the embarrassment she might feel'. Charlie thought this was a good description of her reservations. Margison also had doubts about whether Charlie would feel comfortable in group therapy: 'maintaining a coping front would make this difficult for her'. Lapworth also considered a period of group psychotherapy might follow individual therapy, although he did not indicate that he felt Charlie might have any reservations about this.

Claire Wintram and Frank Margison both identified Charlie's feelings about the abortion of her baby, and suggested the tenth anniversary as one of the reasons for her seeking therapy now. The abortion was mentioned right at the end of the first interview. It was like one of those door handle remarks that are often so significant. Although it was clearly not the only reason why Charlie sought help, revealing it as the interview finished may have been an indication of how painful an experience this had been. It was almost an afterthought, but Wintram had picked up on it strongly (and Margison marginally less so) as an experience Charlie had not worked through and was still grieving. There was one sentence that Charlie found particularly helpful: 'She needs to know that she didn't kill her baby'. She explained that she did not feel guilty about having had the abortion itself. What she did feel guilty about was that it was a decision that had to be made at all, because she felt she may have killed the baby earlier – there may have been something she did or did not do that caused the malformation in the child. She recalled that she was stripping a door around the time she became pregnant, and she may have absorbed some lead from the paint. She could not help that, of course, but there was a sense in which she obviously believed she might have killed her baby. Abortion itself was not an emotive moral issue – it was just not a good solution. It was a personally (rather than a morally) emotional issue for Charlie. She acknowledged that it might be helpful talking with other women who had experienced similar feelings, but she did not *know* that. What was very helpful in Claire Wintram's response was her confirmation of Charlie keeping 'poignant mementoes' like the identity bracelet, and her admiration for the way in which Charlie 'keeps alive the spirit of her dead baby' was 'very kind'.

Overall, Charlie had less to comment upon in this account than in the others. She was as positive towards Claire as towards most of the other therapists; the real difference in her feedback was that there was nothing she wished to correct in Claire's account.

The effect of the project on Charlie

At the beginning of our last meeting, Charlie described in more detail what she had just hinted at when we met for the second set of interviews, that she had been depressed. She now explained how deeply depressed she had been, about a month after the initial interview (before she would have received the transcript). This lasted for three or four months, coinciding both with the tenth anniversary of her abortion and her birthday, although she did not realize this at the time. She was partly prepared for this, because she remembered I had told her that the interview might well stir up many feelings she had not experienced for a long time. Coming out of the depression, it had made her wary of thinking too much about herself. She explained that although she knew she could get in touch with me, she had not done so for a number of reasons, the first of which was that such depression makes her apathetic. The second reason was because she felt that it might interfere with the process of the project if she sought help at that point. Her third reason, expressed with that delightful humour which Charlie from time to time exhibits, was her worry what it would do to her therapist, for her to present every now and again the thoughts and wisdom of six other therapists!

One of her concerns in taking part was that she might find out something about herself which she did not know. With one exception this had not happened. The exception was the realization that there was possibly more grief for her father than she had yet been allowed, or allowed herself, to express. As I have recorded above in the response to Margison's chapter, she was afraid that this grief might overwhelm her.

One of the signs of change in her was in her reading. After her abortion she gave up reading any kind of serious literature, not because it was too painful, but because it did not do anything for her and she could not handle that. Now she had started reading poetry again, especially Shelley, because although he is a Romantic, 'he is also cerebral'. As referred to already, she intends to read Radclyffe Hall's *The Well of Unhappiness* (Frank Margison's recommendation).

When she first came, Charlie mentioned quite a lot of rows with her then thirteen-year-old daughter. Those had stopped, and in many ways they were very close, 'closer than we have been for years'. She wondered whether one of the reasons why she got on so well with her was because she is in many ways the same age as her (as the reference above to Pirani's and Lapworth's questions and her age also suggest). They had similar interests such as music (although different rock bands!), and in society and moral issues. Charlie was trying to get the balance right between allowing her daughter to enjoy her adolescence in the way she was not permitted to herself by her own mother, and yet retaining the necessary limits that a parent needs to maintain to help an adolescent to grow. Charlie also thought she was now a better mother. She thought much more before responding to her children: 'I am now more likely to listen to what's going on. I take the time to think about it before I say or do anything, in a way I didn't before. I notice that in my relationship with all my children. I am conscious of what mothering can do'.

The therapists taking part in this book rightly express their reservations about the comparatively brief amount of information they have about Charlie, and the real disadvantage of not being present with her in the room. Perhaps such reservations were in part an insurance against criticisms the reader might make of them, although I have to record that not only Charlie, but I too, felt that their observations were very rich, full of insight, and uncannily accurate despite not having met her face to face. Their perceptions at one remove give some hope to supervisors, that they – who also receive the material of a session at second-hand (not withstanding the reflective possibilities of the supervisory process) – nevertheless can make a positive contribution to the furtherance of understanding. The other point to be made about our therapists' reservations is that if the material gathered here is only the result of a few sessions, it is more than most therapists receive after an initial assessment; and therapists take what may turn out to be momentous decisions as to what to offer clients on the basis of more limited knowledge than our therapists have been able to acquire here. Again the evidence here appears to be that good therapists, even with limited information, possess an ability to make useful formulations. Their accuracy, of course, can only be tested over a much longer period.

I wondered, towards the end of the last meeting in which we reviewed the work of six therapists, in what ways Charlie had been hurt in the process. She said that one of the first things that hurt her was receiving the transcript of the first session, which I had headed as the title of this book: *Charlie – An Unwanted Child*? But in her usual way, she thought about it, and soon afterwards thought, 'That's absolutely right! Why didn't I think of that before?' Indeed, before seeing that title, Charlie had all sorts of excuses for the behaviour of her mother: that she was a difficult child, that she was a burden, that her mother wanted a boy, that she wanted a pretty girl, or a girl who would be the way she wanted her to be, so that 'if I had been different she would have been different. All the while I was thinking, it was me she didn't want'. But just reading the phrase, she had realized that her mother did not want any child, and that even if she had been a boy, or different, or the daughter she wanted, it would still not have been good enough. It came as a shock at first to think of herself as an unwanted child, but after a few days she thought, 'If I had thought of that twenty years ago it might have helped – it took a lot of the responsibility from me. The fact that I was there at all was the problem'.

Charlie had also been concerned to think that she had anger within her. But again thinking about it she had begun to realize that if she could get the anger out of her more, and express it, she would not keeping turning it inwards as guilt. She was also much more aware of the significance of the past, not just in herself, but in others she knows as well.

'In Search of a Therapist': six therapists offered Charlie their help. As Charlie put it, 'I'm utterly spoilt for choice. In a sense I don't deserve this'. All had something to recommend them, and she felt she could probably work with any of them. I asked her, if she had the resources to go into therapy, had taking part in this made her feel she would like that? 'Yes, very much so'. She had resisted asking for help in the period when she had been so depressed, for reasons I have already outlined, but also because she wasn't sure at that time that she wanted therapy. Now she felt she would like it 'in the near future'. She wanted 'to thank all of them for the time with me and for me, and I do appreciate that. All of them have said something which I found helpful. All of them have had tremendous insight'.

I wondered also what it had been like to be engaged in the process:

It's actually been quite therapeutic in itself. I don't normally talk about myself and my feelings in quite this way. I was surprised how good the first time – just how good it felt. This person is listening to me for a whole hour! It felt good to get it all out. Having said it out loud and having it reflected back at me in a different way and in ways that I hadn't thought of, made me feel a lot better about myself. And having six people appear to like me – I wasn't prepared for that. It was reassuring – perhaps I could tell someone about my problems, and they wouldn't say, 'Go away, stop wasting my time'. It would be quite nice.

But what were the difficulties?

A lot of the questions I didn't expect, and I felt very inadequate, that I wasn't explaining it very well. I didn't realize how much other people mattered to me. I hadn't realized how much I didn't want to let people down. I learned things about myself I didn't know, and most of it was good, but it was scary finding out just how scared I am of the grief, and I wonder if perhaps that put me off . . .

Charlie finished with a story which was just as expressive as any of those she had told me and the other therapists:

I wouldn't say that I was arachnophobic, but I don't like spiders. My daughter yesterday said that she wanted a pet tarantula. I immediately freaked. I thought, 'I'll never feel safe in my house again'. So I said jokingly, 'OK, you can have a spider, but in exchange, for my birthday I want that Spider Friendly Programme at London Zoo, which I read about'. One of the things that puts you off that is that one day they take you into the spider house, and they present you with the biggest, furriest, hairiest, leggiest tarantula in the zoo, and I can't actually face that. Although on one level I am attracted to therapy, I know that ultimately I'm going to have to come face to face with that spider. The spider is my grief and my anger. And I think I'm even more scared now than I was before, because it's more explicit now, and I'm more aware of it now.

I assured Charlie that I thought that in therapy she would have more control over what she revealed to herself and her therapist than she had had in this process. I and the therapists had asked much, and had no doubt opened up areas for which she was not prepared.

Charlie said she had learned much, about therapy as well as about herself. She had many insights, thinking about aspects of herself in ways she had not experienced before. 'Are you different from two years ago?', I asked. 'Oh, I think so. I'm much more aware now. I've set out on a course of self-discovery. I've learned so much more about myself, but I've also learned quite a bit about therapy. And knowledge is power'. She felt this knowledge would enable her to face a therapist or counsellor, if not on equal at least on less inhibiting terms.

Those two aspects of knowledge, both about herself and also about therapy, is a good reminder to us – her readers and listeners – that in sharing her story with us Charlie has helped us, through our knowledge of her, to learn more about therapy as well.